Praise for *Who Do You Want to Be?*:

'Genuinely original and helpful. I read it in one sitting –
pencil and notebook in hand'
Kathryn Davies, Associate Director, Procter & Gamble

'As a working professional and mother in mid-career,
Nicola has helped me to understand that I can live my life
orientated towards my values and dreams without fear of
the consequence of change. I only wish I had discovered
this twenty years ago'
Louise Smalley, Human Resources Director, Whitbread
Group PLC

ABOUT THE AUTHOR

Nicola Bunting is a personal and professional coach and founder of the international bespoke coaching company La Vita Nuova. She is one of only 1 per cent of coaches to have attained the Master Certified Coach Credential and her clients include executives, celebrities, business leaders and people who want to get more out of their life and work.

Before she trained as a coach, Nicola worked as a university professor in the USA and UK and has a PhD in English Literature from Emory University, Atlanta, Georgia, USA.

For more information about Nicola and her work, visit her website: www.la-vita-nuova.com. You can also follow her on Twitter: @LVNcoaching.

WHO DO YOU WANT TO BE?

How to Embrace Change and Live Your Dream

DR NICOLA BUNTING

piatkus

PIATKUS

First published in Great Britain in 2012 by Piatkus

ISBN 978-0-7499-5418-5

Illustration on p. 141: Copyright © 2012 The Enneagram Institute.
All Rights Reserved. Used with permission. www.EnneagramInstitute.com.

Typeset in Esprit by M Rules
Printed and bound in Great Britain by
Clays Ltd, St Ives plc

Papers used by Piatkus are from well-managed forests
and other responsible sources.

MIX
Paper from
responsible sources
FSC® C104740

Piatkus
An imprint of
Little, Brown Book Group
100 Victoria Embankment
London EC4Y 0DY

An Hachette UK Company
www.hachette.co.uk

www.piatkus.co.uk

To Christopher, with all my love
always on all of your journeys

CONTENTS

ACKNOWLEDGEMENTS

Thank you to my agent Antony Topping of Greene and Heaton for your faith in me, your help and insights with my book proposal and your general brilliance. You are a pleasure to work with. Thanks also to my editor, Anne Lawrance at Piatkus, for being so supportive, encouraging, and delightful along every step of the journey of writing this book. And a heartfelt thank you to all my wonderful coaching clients, past, present, and future. You inspire me every day.

Introduction

Midway in our life's journey, I went astray from the straight road and woke to find myself alone in a dark wood
THE DIVINE COMEDY, DANTE ALIGHIERI

For Christmas 2009, Harrods put on a special *Wizard of Oz* display. There was a run on sales of their 'ruby slippers' – only not the children's sizes, which remained on the shelves in abundance, but the adult ones. Does this reflect the times we live in, and our desire for a 'quick fix'? It certainly suggests that a lot of us would like to change our lives, click our heels and be somewhere else ...

Change is part of our everyday experience, whether it's the immediate shock of suddenly being made redundant and asked to clear your desk, or the challenge of choosing to change your career or ending your marriage. But the way in which you handle change can influence whether it's fantastic or terrible and, ultimately, how happy you are in life.

———

The secret to navigating change successfully lies in how you respond to it. You can use the energy of change to propel yourself forward on an exhilarating adventure, or you can resist, fight, allow yourself to be threatened, even defeated, by the wave of change.

Imagine change and challenge as a big, powerful wave moving towards you. Rather than feeling scared, overwhelmed or powerless, how would it feel if you were a surfer, anticipating the wave as part of an exciting adventure?

What comes to mind when you picture a graceful surfer on the crest of a wave ... exhilaration, harmony, connectedness, balance? What if you could approach your life with the same qualities, poised and ready to catch your next wave, *to become part of it*, to seize the extraordinary opportunities in front of you? Are you ready to deal with your next wave?

Being afraid to live life differently can result in blocked energy and boredom, so sometimes we need to initiate change ourselves in order to move our lives forward. But how do we learn the life-surfing skills we need to ready ourselves for turning challenge or stuckness into opportunity and success?

People today are increasingly looking for direction, focus and meaning – for a path through Dante's dark wood. Naturally, we yearn to identify genuine and sustainable sources of inspiration and guidance, to find answers to the important questions about what it means to be happy, to be successful, to be truly authentic. And with global changes forcing more and more successful mid-career individuals to examine their options, change their jobs, careers, often even their way of living and their assumptions about life, the time has come for a practical, intelligent exploration of what it really takes to turn challenges, confusion and crises into brilliant opportunities for success.

Who Do You Want To Be? How to Embrace Change and Live Your Dream is your guide to that journey of discovery. Whether you're an ambitious professional woman with a young family, struggling to reconcile and feel good about your different roles, or a man in mid-career, already on the board, but feeling that something is still missing, or a finance professional who needs to change career and maybe life paths, this book is for you. It is for everyone who is feeling uncertain about their current personal or professional situation and who wants to find opportunity and success through trials and crisis. It will give you a framework for understanding the nature of your challenges and the scope of your options, and will help you along the journey to happiness, fulfilment and, at times, even bliss. Inspired by years of working with professionals who are deliberately seeking to do just that, it is, above all, an exciting and pragmatic step-by-step guide for anyone who is, for whatever reason, unable to access one-on-one coaching with me, yet who is committed to turning challenges into opportunities.

WHY YOU'RE HERE

Did you wake up this morning feeling clear, confident, happy and focused about your day and about where your life is going? Or did you feel tired, apprehensive, maybe even hung over – literally or otherwise? Did you have butterflies about the day ahead or was your stomach in knots? Were you feeling blocked, stuck or confused? Did you ask yourself: how did I get here? Or, more importantly: how do I get *there*?

Sometimes, a plane to Chicago is diverted to New York; that shopping trip to Paris on the Eurostar is scuppered by the snowdrift outside your front door; plans you've made for your life, your career, your relationships, your family and your finances can suddenly need dramatic adjustment. You need a Plan B, sometimes, with little or no notice.

Change is inevitable for all of us. It can lead to conflict, disappointment and crisis, or it can lead to exciting adventures, growth and new opportunity. Whether it's ultimately a positive or a negative change depends on how we approach it, how we handle it.

Why have you bought this book today? Perhaps you've been made redundant and are feeling shell-shocked and stunned, confused about your next professional step and the implications for your life. Perhaps you're in the middle of a stressful divorce and are struggling to make sense of

———

the emotional wasteland you feel trapped in. Perhaps you've been married for several years and don't feel as happy as you expected in your relationship, but feel too scared to examine this feeling. Or perhaps you're confronting positive change – say, a job offer in another country, the prospect of getting engaged to be married – but are not sure how to react. Maybe your successful career isn't inspiring you any more, and you long to change direction towards something more fulfilling, but aren't sure what. How can you navigate this uncertainty into the satisfying career you want? You might have the professional and personal life you thought you wanted, but feel miserable and lost, yet unsure of what that means and what you can do about it. Maybe you feel overwhelmed and conflicted, struggling to combine a demanding career with being a mother of small children, but can't imagine a way forward.

While I don't know the specific reason why you're reading this book right now, I do know that if you want to navigate change successfully, to turn a potential crisis into an exciting adventure and create a life that reflects who you really are and what you most want, you're in the right place.

I have spent the last twelve years working with people just like you, to help them create order and clarity from chaos, to deal with change and make it work for them and to build authentic, meaningful, joyful lives and careers – no matter however confused and blocked they might have been when we first met. And what I've shown them is that it's often the points in our lives where we face the greatest changes and challenges that provide the most exciting opportunities to redesign our lives so that they reflect what we most want and value.

The changes and potential crises you may be facing are really your own call to adventure – your opportunity to develop, learn and leap forward on all levels. This book will show you how, giving you a road map to your dream destination, whatever that may look like to you.

Above all, you will find that this book is a practical step-by-step guide to managing change. My tactics are results-orientated – as you will see with the help of client examples – and I'm confident that the tools I give you will work.

THE CALL TO ADVENTURE

I like to break change down into two categories: external and internal. External change is when something happens to which you must respond; internal change is prompted by a feeling that you want to live differently – both are a call to adventure.

The adventure (because it is an adventure!) forces you,

like Dorothy leaving Kansas, to leave a familiar place and venture into the unknown. The route is often challenging, difficult, confusing, sometimes lonely; to navigate it successfully, you need self-awareness, resilience and strong mental, emotional, physical and spiritual reserves.

The internal call could be a feeling of constriction, claustrophobia, limitation, even flatness or unhappiness – an 'Is this all there is?' sensation. Surely life could be fuller, happier, more inspiring. Until this point, life has had its own momentum: school, university, work, setting up home, creating relationships, getting promoted, perhaps starting a family. Then suddenly, one Monday morning, you wake up feeling bored at the prospect of the week ahead. Or you reach whatever personal or professional goal you'd set yourself, only to feel a bit 'so-what'-ish when you get there.

An external call is often a situational development that necessitates action: you are made redundant and need to find a new job, even explore a new career; your marriage suddenly disintegrates; your youngest child leaves home for university; or you suffer a bereavement or significant physical illness. Whatever the external trigger, you are faced with change – or a call to adventure, if you choose to see it in that light.

This book is your personal road map to make your call to adventure successful. I wish I had found such a resource at earlier points in my own life. Having changed careers

WHO DO YOU WANT TO BE?

twice before finding my dream job in my thirties, I had many moments when I felt really lost and confused – conflicted about other people's expectations of me, and about the competing and, apparently, irreconcilable claims between work, my young family and my desire for time to relax and have fun. I spent years in a marriage feeling not entirely happy, but unsure as to what, if anything, I could do about it. I also lived in several countries, including the USA, Italy and the UK, and each relocation introduced a completely different life to which I had to adjust. Now in my forties, having successfully navigated these rapids, I apply with my coaching clients the same framework for taking advantage of change that I used myself.

MIDLIFE CRISIS? OR MIDLIFE OPPORTUNITY?

Midlife is when you reach the top of the ladder and find that it was against the wrong wall.

JOSEPH CAMPBELL

I find with my life-coaching clients that it's most often at midlife – in their thirties to fifties – that they are called on this adventure of self-discovery.

It's natural to re-evaluate personal and work choices at this time of life. You understand yourself better and what makes you happy. And when your personal and professional circumstances change, that inevitably makes you reflect and reassess.

But the term 'midlife crisis' is a misnomer for what is really the exciting and profound potential for development and discovery that we all face at this point in our lives. The midlife 'crisis' needs to be totally rebranded in light of the fact that so many people in their thirties, forties and fifties are determined to find a meaning in life that will inspire them, to discover the values that will carry them through the remainder of their lives. With the self-understanding and life experience that such people already have, they are all the better equipped to tackle change successfully and to turn it to advantage, becoming more poised, ready, self-aware, intentional and powerful.

Often, we tend to seek stability and reassurance outside, and when the unexpected happens, find ourselves lost, disorientated and uncertain as to where to turn or what to do next. When this happens to you, rather than try to find meaning in the outer changeable circumstances of your life, the way forward is to cultivate inner stability, self-understanding, equilibrium, resilience and increased personal reserves of health, energy, and inspiration.

A successful transition to the second half of your life

allows you to become a fuller, more realised, more conscious version of your former self. A failure to move forward and develop in this way can often result in mid-life ennui, limitation, frustration, confusion. If you alter your perspective and focus on who you want to be, how you want to feel, the life you want to live – in short, if you take charge of change from the inside out – options open up. And by understanding exactly where you want to be, you can see more clearly what you need to do to get there.

YOU'RE INVITED . . .

I'm inviting you on a journey from here to there – from OK, good enough, unsettled or unsure, to fantastic, fulfilled, focused and fun. And this book will be your guide. It's not a change-your-life-in-a-weekend book, but you can certainly *start* changing your life *this* weekend.

In my experience of working with people to help them make exciting transformations in their life, just about anything is possible, but it takes time, focus and effort. Quick fixes are often short-term hype that seem to provide answers, but don't give you the substantive long-lasting results you want – a bit like a fast-food Chinese takeaway that's full of MSG and seems to fill you up, but which leaves you feeling hungry and unsatisfied just a short while later.

By applying the framework and using the toolkit I provide in this book, you will be able to make real, sustainable, significant changes in your life. It's not a quick fix, but a passage with structure, direction and tried-and-tested results. It is not only your valuable guide for the here and now, but also a resource that you can pick up in a few years' time when you're confronted with another opportunity or challenge. It will give you equally great results each time you use it, whatever the situation that prompts you to revisit.

NOW LET'S BEGIN

Let today be the first day of your new year, whether it's January the first, or April or October, and cast aside whatever excuses you might have for putting it off. The first thing you're *not* going to do about your problems is to run away from them. The danger in running away is that you could well end up somewhere that's just as unsatisfactory as where you are right now. If you race as fast as possible to whatever alternative seems to present itself, you'll be missing a precious opportunity to understand and proactively create something that's spectacular and wonderful and right for yourself.

So start by taking some time out to understand where and who you are right now, and where and who you want to be.

I was speaking to a new client recently – a talented thirty-something media executive, who found herself really unhappy in her current role and was desperate to move somewhere, anywhere, just to get out of it and to get away. This is common: often our inclination when we feel stuck, blocked or unhappy is to take any action that makes us feel we're doing something positive. But without proper reflection, understanding and clarity, we may end up making a mistake or, at best, settling for OK, rather than special.

You need to start with a really clear understanding of what you want – what's right for the unique individual you are at this particular point and place in your life. To gain this clarity, you need to stop running away, stay still and reflect. You must create an inspiring, focused map of your dream destination and a plan for how you're going to get there in the easiest and most enjoyable way possible.

The first part of this book – 'Invitation to the Journey' – is how you do this. And the time you'll spend reading about how to turn crisis to opportunity, to make change work to your advantage, is a valuable investment in your ultimate success.

Once you've understood the framework, you'll be rolling up your sleeves and getting stuck into the practical part of the book: 'Getting Where You Want to Go'. Here, you will set aside a day for yourself – your Personal Vision Day. It could be a Saturday or Sunday, or any day you take out for yourself during the week. During this day, you'll explore how to understand more deeply who you really are and who you have the potential to be; in other words, what you would see if you could look at your personality objectively, from the outside in, rather than the inside out. Understanding more fully who you really are shows you more clearly what you need in order to be truly fulfilled, as well as the best way to achieve your goals. On your Personal Vision Day, you'll create your own toolkit of successful approaches and useful insights to assist you on your journey to your very own technicolour Oz or maybe for your return to Kansas, or a different part of Kansas – whatever's right for you.

You're at the threshold of your own new year for creating the fulfilling life and work that you dream of. Let's build it together, one step at a time, starting today.

———

PART I
INVITATION TO
THE JOURNEY

CHAPTER I

Following the Call

There are moments in life when everything changes. Sometimes, the change is immediate: something happens, something big, and the whole landscape shifts and we find ourselves somewhere else. Other times, the change is gradual, almost imperceptible, until one day we wake up, either literally or metaphorically, to find that the new day demands a different way of being. We feel stuck, sad, blocked and confused, and we know we can't continue in the same way. We know we have to do something different to save our own life and move it forward, towards happiness.

Behind the scenes, something interesting and unexpectedly wonderful is being prepared for us (though it may not feel especially wonderful at the time). We are being called to adventure, invited on a journey, called forward from our

---

old way of living or being and into a new world. Sometimes, it's not just one external change that propels us out from the familiar into a scary world. Sometimes, lots of things can change and even appear to fall apart at once. Writer Anne Lamott makes a beautifully reassuring point about this scenario in her book *Traveling Mercies*: 'When a lot of things start going wrong all at once, it is to protect something big and lovely that is trying to get itself born, and this something needs for you to be distracted so that it can be born as perfectly as possible.' The trick is to focus on what new possibilities may be waiting for you on the other side of your adventure.

When you read the words 'call to adventure', you may not immediately identify with them or view whatever is happening to you in that light. Adventure often brings to mind something that is glamorous and exciting – like a hike through the waterfalls of Hawaii or climbing the ancient temples of Machu Picchu – and something that may require significant financial investment. And when you're in the midst of the grit and often mundane-seeming realities of your own life, it is almost impossible to gain a clear perspective of where you're heading or where you have the potential to be. You can't see the possibilities behind the problem. You're so focused on the door that is closing that you ignore the magic doors opening all around you.

———

At any given moment, you may be guided by a default map based on past experiences and preconceptions or narrow thinking. I see this shortsightedness all the time with my coaching clients, and it's very natural, given the limitations imposed by living life from the inside out. But if you try to relax, reframe and expand your vision, the real picture of possibility emerges like a kaleidoscope rearranging its pattern into something beautiful.

WHAT IS A CALL TO ADVENTURE?

A call to adventure is when we're summoned to go on a journey or quest. This is the pattern: we leave our familiar existence to venture forward into something unknown. On the journey we're stretched out of our familiar comfort zone, we learn, we grow, we face challenges, danger, virtual or metaphorical battles even. With courage, focus, commitment and willingness to step into the new and uncertain, and with helpers along the way, we overcome our challenges – we learn, develop our understanding and gain magical treasure which we then take back into our lives to infuse them with passion, power and success.

Children's stories (and adults' too, for that matter) are full of calls to adventure. Think of Bilbo Baggins being summoned by the wizard Gandalf to leave his comfortable hobbit hole and venture forth on a dangerous quest to kill the dragon and rescue the hoard of gold and precious stones in its lair. Or Dorothy's house being transported in a tornado, taking her from the black and white world of Kansas and catapulting her into the technicolour world of Oz, where her helpers, the Tin Man, the Scarecrow and the Cowardly Lion – each with a quest of their own – accompany her down the yellow-brick road in search of the all-powerful wizard who can grant their wishes . . .

We are all familiar with adventure-story plots that follow these trajectories, but usually struggle to see our own lives with the same clarity. But, in fact, our own quest patterns are the same as in the stories. A call to adventure is simply an invitation to renew, invigorate and deepen our lives – a call to greater happiness, self-understanding, peace and confidence. It's a call, I believe, from our higher or best self to pull us forward into the full and profound life we are capable of – a call to go from Muggle to magic, from the wardrobe to the snowy landscape of Narnia. But the invitation doesn't always come beautifully presented, ready to display on the mantelpiece, and we don't always recognise it as the opportunity it really is.

I've seen so many calls to adventure over the years with my coaching clients; they are often what makes people get in touch with me in the first place. And I've been privileged to accompany my clients on countless extraordinary adventures, and see them reap some spectacular rewards as a result.

I sometimes see my coaching role as that of the travel guide in my clients' adventures, helping them to clarify where they want to go, and preparing them, as far as possible, to get there safely. Of course, this is a metaphor; I find it an appealing image to picture my client and I getting ready together to embark on a quest through the dark woods.

TWO TYPES OF CALL TO ADVENTURE

So that you can understand the nature and significance of your own call more clearly, let me explain about the two different types of invitation:

1. Something happens to you

This type of call is unmistakably obvious. Something external happens to you and your life that throws you unceremoniously out of your comfort zone into a cold and confusing place.

Often, a big loss precipitates change, challenge and sometimes even crisis. Examples are job loss or redundancy, marriage or relationship breakdown, your youngest child leaving home, bereavement or serious illness. Positive changes can be catalysts too, launching you on an adventure in just the same way – developments such as moving in with your partner or getting married, starting a new job or, indeed, changing career, having a baby, moving house, starting university, turning thirty, forty, fifty or sixty (or any other noteworthy age milestone), significant weight loss, falling in love ... the list is almost endless. Change creates a rite of passage into new possibilities. Even the start of a new year can herald a wonderful new beginning for you, your life and your work, if you choose this for yourself.

My point is that any significant external change in your life can propel you forward into an exciting journey if you allow it to. Faced with hurdles, we have the option of jumping over them. Similarly, we can react to a dramatic external change from a place of strength, inquiry, positive intent and open-mindedness, or we can retract into a closed place of fear and denial, where we feel powerless and our options diminish daily. Put simply, we can be reactive or proactive.

2. Something happens inside you

In this second, perhaps rather more subtle call to adventure, the invitation to the journey arises from an internal feeling, rather than an external challenge, jolt or shake-up.

For example, you may increasingly catch yourself feeling a bit odd on Sundays. Perhaps you used to have a happy sense of anticipation on a Sunday evening, thinking about what the new work week would bring, but now notice you're feeling quite unexcited, maybe a bit anxious, apprehensive or even filled with dread.

You may have been travelling along the trajectory from anticipation to dread for many years, and realise very suddenly that you're not enjoying your job or your career any more and that it's time for a change. Or perhaps you're quite self-aware and noticed the gradual changes earlier on in the process.

According to Mappiness, an app which maps happiness across the UK, and is part of a research project at the London School of Economics, Mondays and Tuesdays are the least happy days of the week, with Friday and Saturday the most happy. That means an awful lot of people are not actively enjoying their working lives, which seems like a sad waste of potential happiness and fulfilment.

Then there's marriage. Maybe you've noticed that you feel lonely in your marriage – that you don't feel joy or love any more when you think about your partner, just sad and a little empty. You recognise somewhere inside you that your relationship isn't fulfilling any more, you feel hopeless and increasingly disenchanted at the prospect of investing more time and energy into it.

———

Interestingly, with relationships, as I sometimes find with my coaching clients, it's quite common to attribute an internal sensation of block or dissatisfaction to your intimate relationships. In other words you may place unfair blame on your relationship for your own boredom or depression. By putting more into your own personal development (and *then* into cultivating your relationship), it's very possible to transform a less than thrilling relationship into something dynamic and fulfilling. Sometimes, of course, two people have grown in such different ways that their journeys almost inevitably pull them apart. But not always. It is possible to reconnect, even if your journeys have taken you in temporarily different directions.

For now, though, don't assume that because you think you're feeling a call to adventure, to leave your long-term relationship, it means an end is inevitable and the only solution or way forward is to get out. Generally, with relationships, as with other areas of life, we're not talking about leaving (losing, or risking) something excellent for something that is hypothetically, theoretically perfect. There is a very definite distinction between learning, growing and developing and escapism.

Sometimes, the need for change and growth can manifest as a sort of ennui, boredom, restlessness, even depression. All of these feelings may be indications that it's time to go on an adventure to a deeper understanding and awareness – time to invest some energy and attention in your personal development and shine a light on your values and sources of inspiration to see where they might take you. Trying to stay still when your life wants you to spring forward takes a lot of energy, and can show up as a feeling of stuckness, frustration, claustrophobia or sadness. This type of avoidance can lead to deliberately numbing activities, such as overeating, drinking too much, losing yourself in television and computer games or whichever ways you as an individual may have of emotionally checking out.

WHAT A CALL TO ADVENTURE ACTUALLY FEELS LIKE

A call to adventure doesn't always (in fact, often doesn't) feel like you might imagine it would. You might expect to feel excited, inspired, hopeful, energised; and sometimes, you will, especially if you have a positive external call to adventure, such as a new job, a new year or a house move, for example.

However, for many people it can feel like being in the middle of a dark night or a dark room, where you can't get your bearings. It can feel frightening, disorientating. You don't know quite where you are or even where or who you

---

want to be. You have the feeling that there's a place you need to get to, that there is something potentially wonderful out there for you, but you don't have the road map for your adventure and you don't know where to start or head to. You can feel really lost, anxious, confused, depressed, maybe even panicky, as though you've been thrown out of a comfortable place and into an uncertain waiting room between two worlds. You may find yourself waking up in the early hours, your mind racing, unable to get back to sleep and feeling scared.

It is at this point in their lives that many of my clients approach me, as it is exactly when an expert coach can be especially helpful, providing the perspective with which to see their destination, as well as the tools that will get them there safely.

WHEN ARE YOU MOST LIKELY
TO GET THE CALL?

A call to adventure can arrive at any time. It could be triggered when you're eighteen by leaving home to start university, or at twenty-one, when you're trying to decide on your vocation or looking for your first job, or in your late fifties, by the prospect of retirement.

———

However, in my experience as a long-term life and executive coach, the call to adventure is most likely to strike at midlife, defined most broadly as that period of life from your mid-thirties to your mid-fifties.

CRISIS OR OPPORTUNITY?

We tend to think of a 'midlife crisis' negatively and reductively – disparagingly, in fact. It's thought of as affecting, characteristically, men, most likely in their mid-forties, who, alarmed at the prospect (or reality) of losing their hair and their youth, react by looking for superficial external quick fixes to make them feel young again – the stereotypical red sports car or leaving their long-term relationship to run away with another woman young enough to be their daughter, for example. Clearly, this kind of scenario is a crisis that can happen at mid-life, and clearly it's not a constructive way to handle a fear of limitation or mortality. The problem, of course, with such superficial apparent solutions, is that they are knee-jerk reactions to change, rather than responses borne of a desire to use change as an opportunity to grow, develop and become more fulfilled. A quick fix can, and often does, lead to more problems.

But the stereotypical image of the midlife crisis is exactly that – a stereotype; and I believe something much more interesting and complex is happening. In reality, men and woman are equally affected by midlife reflectiveness and this actually starts in our thirties. Importantly though, I believe that a midlife crisis is a positive thing. And from experience of coaching many individuals at midlife to new levels of understanding, achievement and happiness, I believe, as mentioned in the Introduction, that the midlife crisis should be rebranded as midlife opportunity.

Think about it like this: imagine you're living in a big, beautiful house with several floors and many different rooms. You're currently occupying the rooms on the ground floor only, which you've furnished and made quite comfortable and pleasant. Imagine the possibilities if you ventured upstairs, opened the unopened doors, brushed the metaphorical cobwebs away, unstuck the windows to let the air in, looked at the light, the potential for creating wonderful new spaces to inhabit, ways to live, perhaps a study, a room for holding parties in, a spare bedroom for guests, a room for a gym ... The scope is endless.

Your life is like that house in a way. You have all kinds of potential, possibilities, spaces inside you, gifts, strengths and unlived lives, all waiting to be stepped into and enjoyed. You just need to discover them, to be prepared to face the unknown and the less known, to see what's there, to experiment with uncertainty, to be open-minded and prepared for delightful surprises.

I find that it's most frequently at the midlife point that we suddenly discover the unlived life within us – that staircase leading to the rooms upstairs. Typically, in childhood and young adulthood we follow a fairly well-defined path and forward-moving trajectory that doesn't require a huge amount of introspection or reflection. Most of our decisions are made for us, and even though we may experiment with independence as we grow older, we generally follow the path that has been defined for us, and we are busy with the external demands of higher education, finding our first (and next) job, falling in love and moving in with our partner or getting married, setting up home, making enough money to get by, having our first child ...

So it's often not until our thirties, at the earliest, that we find we have time to reflect on our lives and consider who and where we are in relation to who and where we think we might want to be. And many people, busy with the demands of a career, making a living, starting a family, don't get to the point of pause and reflection until they reach their forties.

At the same time, there's also a Peter-Pan thing going on, I think. Until midlife, however broadly we define it, we tend to think of ourselves as young and immortal; on some level, getting older and having a finite time to make choices in life doesn't seem very real. Until, that is, something big happens to us (the external call to adventure) or we pause to consider that unsettling feeling that is rising inside us (the internal call).

The psychologist Carl Jung, provides a helpful framework within which to think about what's happening to us at midlife. He refers to the midlife opportunity as 'individuation'. At midlife we are given the chance to become more fully ourselves, to understand the depth and scale of our personality more profoundly, to move into those unexplored rooms of our self and integrate into our conscious awareness those parts of ourselves we may have been ignoring or repressing. The reward for this work of discovery is renewed inspiration, energy, excitement for life and its possibilities. In essence, midlife itself presents us with a call to adventure, an invitation to venture out from the familiar and into the unknown, to find the treasures that represent more profound and joyful life experiences. These opportunities to expand our sense of self will be explored more in the next chapter.

The call to adventure we experience at midlife, whether external or internal, represents a wonderful opportunity for happiness. It is a signal that we have almost certainly outgrown something in our lives and that we're ready for something new and different. It is scary and daunting, but potentially exciting too, if we see it more objectively.

TRUE STORIES

Let me share some true stories with you from my clients'
experiences and my own life. You will see the variety of
ways in which calls to adventure can present themselves
and the fabulous outcomes that can be won by accepting
the invitation.

Susan's story

Recently, I received an email from an old client, Susan,
with the inviting subject line, 'Hurrah!' Her email went like
this: 'What a difference a few years make, huh? I couldn't
be happier to have finally reached my ultimate professional
goal and your help along that path has been invaluable.
Thank you so much for your support!'

Now let me tell you where Susan was two years ago. One
morning she went downstairs to get her coffee and found a
note on the kitchen table. It was from her husband, and it
said that he had decided to leave her – he was on his way to
Canada (at the airport by the time she read the note), and
wanted a divorce. To say Susan was shocked would be a big
understatement. She had been unhappy in her marriage for
some time, although she hadn't realised it was on the verge
of disintegration. Additionally, she wasn't enjoying her job at

all, had an unsupportive boss and some draining colleagues, and very much wanted to move to another company where she would feel more valued and fulfilled. But because it isn't easy to find another senior position in a specialised niche industry, especially when you need to maintain the same level of income, Susan felt trapped. So she found herself in an unexpectedly dark place in all aspects of her life, where she felt lost, unfulfilled, uncertain, let down and scared.

Fast forward two years: with coaching support, focus, dedication, commitment and courage, Susan is happily divorced, enjoying being single and actively dating again. She tells me that so many eligible, interested men are pursuing her that she is now convinced being over forty and single is quite fun! I'm also happy to report that she has a fabulous new job which she was invited to apply for. She is inspired by the values and mission of her new company (is a partner there, in fact), she respects her colleagues and enjoys their company, is earning significantly more than before and is generally thrilled with her life. We're meeting up soon for a celebratory glass of champagne.

John's story

While Susan's call was external in that something happened to her that catapulted her forward, John's call was very much an internal one.

———

John was one of my very first coaching clients, a London solicitor, working for the firm which had been in the family for a few generations. He was uninspired by life as a solicitor in London, to say the least. He was bored, frustrated, stressed, and unhappy, and he wasn't even particularly successful or prosperous in his profession. His cluttered, confused desk was a good metaphor for his state of overwhelm.

At our first coaching meeting, John told me he felt dread at the prospect of another day at work, he was facing tax demands which he didn't think he could meet and he felt trapped in the family firm, unable to conceive of another way to live and work. He was single, a bit isolated, slightly overweight and came across as harried and absent-minded in his demeanour. When I asked him what he most enjoyed in his life at the moment, he lit up and told me that occasionally he went to Wales for the weekend, where he hiked in the hills, played golf and looked at houses – property being another of his interests.

John and I worked together for about two years, focusing on what he most enjoyed, his values, what was holding him back from changing his life and work and what his vision for himself might look like. He worked hard to change his life and his work, and each month he moved forward.

By the end of two years, something dramatic had

happened. John had moved permanently to Wales and given up his profession as a lawyer, closing the London business. He had decided to combine his love for Wales with his interest in property by investing there. He had over a million pounds of property equity and was well on his way to being a millionaire. He was working in a hands-on, engaged way on renovations, his portfolio was thriving and he had lots of free time to go hiking, play golf and be energised by the outdoors. Tellingly, he told me that work didn't feel like work as he had always known it – it actually felt inspiring and enjoyable. You would not have recognised this fulfilled, healthy, confident, prosperous, energised man as the unsuccessful and frustrated London solicitor who had come to me two years previously.

Jane and Ann's story

Whereas Susan's and John's lives both changed dramatically, often the invitation to change your life appears in a more subtle or more specific manner. Clients often come to me with a particular aspiration, something they've wanted to do for years and haven't quite got round to, and ask for coaching help to make it happen. And sometimes, as with Jane and Ann, this can lead to a new career.

Both Jane and Ann had a lifelong dream to become a writer. Both were successful executives – Jane in PR and

Ann a management consultant – who couldn't quite see how they were going to be able, practically, to become full-time writers.

With Jane, our coaching strategy was for her to keep her current job, which she did enjoy, in fact, but change it to four days a week, so that she could devote one day a week entirely to writing. Additionally, we blocked out specific time during the week and weekends that she could use to supplement her writing efforts. We worked simultaneously to increase her confidence and her energy and to help her believe in herself and her writing potential, and gradually her book took shape.

I am happy to say that at the end of the year, Jane found an agent who was delighted to represent her, and she secured a lucrative deal with a major publishing house. This allowed her to leave her PR job and become a full-time novelist.

Jane says: 'I think I've often referred to you as my light-house, my compass and my good fairy, and that's just what you are – the kind, calm and intelligent voice of reason and perspective. Over the last six months, you've guided me through some really substantial life and career changes. It's a great privilege to have your help and support.'

Ann felt torn between her attachment to her management-consulting job, which she felt, realistically, couldn't be done on a part-time schedule, and her desire to write. But whereas Jane initiated the change in her

WHO DO YOU WANT TO BE?

working and writing pattern herself, Ann found herself unexpectedly made redundant. Rather than find the news frightening or unsettling, however, Ann was absolutely delighted, as the redundancy package gave her the financial back-up and practical space she needed in order to be able to start writing full-time. Ann has now published several e-books and has won a writing award. She recently wrote to me:

> I LOVE my new career. I adore the freedom to do what I want and when I want to do it. I can work with my body's rhythm now, i.e. get up WITHOUT an alarm clock, write late into the night, take days off when I need them. Thank you so much, Nicola. You supported me through a very stressful and difficult period in my life. Your coaching helped me make a career change from management consulting to writing. Three years later, I'm not only far happier and fulfilled, I also have seven published books, nine more contracted, two currently being worked on and enough ideas for quite a few more.

Both women now thoroughly enjoy spending their days doing what they love, expressing themselves creatively and receiving recognition and appreciation from their publishers and readers. They have both told me that they sometimes feel a sense of unreality that they can really be making their living doing something they love so much and that often they feel they need to pinch themselves, as it all seems too good to be true.

Jasmine's story

Jasmine came to me at a point when her life had changed to such an extent that she felt quite lost and confused. She had given up a successful banking career in the City in order to stay at home with her two children. After ten years at home, she felt it was time to relaunch her career, but with no desire to return to the City, she didn't know where to start. She knew that she wanted a flexible job that would allow her to spend time with her children, but wasn't sure what would be fun, stimulating and feasible to break into in her forties.

Working together, Jasmine and I focused on identifying what inspired and excited her, who she wanted to work with and what she wanted from her future work and lifestyle. We came to the conclusion that starting her own business was the route to a flexible and dynamic working life – one that would give her the autonomy to decide her own goals, hours and desired income, as well as allow her to work with her ideal clients. Interior design was an area she had always been passionate about, and she was often complimented on her creativity and flair. Here's what happened next, in Jasmine's own words:

———

I had to dig deep within myself, challenge myself with some pretty big, yet fundamental questions. The process, with Nicola's calm and encouraging guidance, was amazingly practical and straightforward. Each week, another light bulb went on, another hurdle was jumped over, another blockage overcome. Every little step was more cathartic and energising than the last. I gained personal clarity and realised my career had to fit me and my life, not the other way round. A very different approach from that which I had followed during a fifteen-year banking career in three countries! I retrained as an interior designer and set up a business focusing on property styling (improving your home to accommodate changing needs or taste) and property staging (setting a 'stage' for rental or sale). Our clients include an *X Factor* judge and a pair of estranged and reunited lovers who finally decided to move in together at the age of seventy-five!

The tools that I learned working with Nicola have been invaluable. Sitting at my desk before our work together I felt totally overwhelmed, aimless and somewhat unfulfilled, despite being a happy person at the core. I knew my life could be so much more, but how?

I am in a totally different place now and one I am at peace with – a place of honesty, clarity and balance. As will all of us, life will continue to offer me challenges, and it is ultimately only I who can change them into opportunities.

Thank you Nicola for teaching me how.

Other individuals I've worked with over the years have made less dramatic changes in their life and work, but have used the coaching journey to develop their professional awareness and success, to learn how to become more balanced, fulfilled, aware and energised personally, and to learn then how to apply this development to their professional life. Occasionally, that has meant changing careers, but more typically, the personal and professional development initiated by the call to adventure leads to working more successfully on several levels in their current role, be that a promotion within their company or moving on to a more senior role in another one.

Practically every week, I receive emails from former clients, telling me about promotions and new jobs. They are always delighted with the positive developments they've experienced, and usually attribute them to the work they did on themselves along our coaching journey.

Here, for example, is what Alan wrote recently:

My coaching with Nicola has been enormously helpful in my personal development overall and in moving me forward professionally over a short time span.

———

About three years ago, in my mid-forties, I started to take stock of my life and concluded there was nothing to complain about: nice, well-paying job, good relationship, lovely apartment, great lifestyle with many foreign trips and exotic holidays. The point that nagged at me was that things were actually a little too cushy, I didn't feel I was exerting myself and felt I was a little too young to start to coast towards (early) retirement. Something was missing; life wasn't particularly challenging and, ultimately, a little frustrating. At that moment, a very dear friend mentioned to me that he was working with Nicola Bunting and felt he was getting huge benefit out of doing so. He highly recommended her and said he felt that working with Nicola was something I should be doing too.

Mapping out with Nicola my emotional and spiritual DNA, raising my self-awareness and understanding my existential drivers and values was hugely beneficial in putting me on a clear path towards a much more gratifying life, more profound relationships and a career change which I would not have contemplated, let alone dared to undertake, without her help. That career change in the autumn of 2007 has led to a rapid promotion to head the non-US business of my firm with responsibilities spanning the globe and operations in Europe, Asia and Australia. I don't think I would have seen myself capable of doing this even a few months ago!

My story

Calls to adventure rarely arrive only once in a lifetime. We are all faced with several significant invitations towards positive change at many points in our lives.

Although still in my forties, when I reflect back on my life so far it sometimes feels as if I've already lived lots of very different lives since I was born in the swinging sixties! I've gone through several significant changes of direction, leaving careers, life paths, countries – I've lived in Italy, England (first London and now Bath) and the USA (in New England, New York, Minnesota and the very deep south) – and personal relationships, making choices which have ultimately led me to feeling the way I do right now: incredibly happy and appreciative of my blessings, with a career and life I adore.

At university, there wasn't really something I longed to do career-wise, and I found this lack of clarity a bit troubling. I did a vocational career test, which told me my top career choice was to be a pilot. That didn't help much, especially as I was putting off even learning to drive a car at the time, as the thought of driving made me nervous!

I decided to pursue a marketing/business career, and was

WHO DO YOU WANT TO BE?

delighted to be offered several management trainee opportunities in exciting companies.

We need to backtrack a little here though, as I have to
confess that a year earlier, at the University of York, where
I was enjoying my BA course in English Literature, I did
actually turn down my first real call to adventure. There
were some glamorous Californian exchange students at the
university, and they inspired me to apply for an exchange
year abroad for my second year at York. I applied to the
University of California at Berkeley and was very excited
to be offered a place and a full scholarship too. I was
thrilled at the academic opportunities Berkeley would offer
(it had a fabulous reputation in English), and probably
even more overjoyed at the prospect of living in San
Francisco for a year, as I had always been drawn to going
there. But I'm somewhat embarrassed to tell you that I
decided not to go and turned down the offer. Why, I hear
you ask? Well, I had lots of excuses, as we so often do in
such situations (I was going out with a gorgeous boy who
didn't want me to go, and I was a bit concerned that I
might not have enough money, etc.). But the bottom line,
of course, is that I turned down the invitation to adventure
and stayed where I was out of fear, though I didn't see it
that way at the time. (In the next chapter I'll explain more
about why we turn down such opportunities/challenges,
and what the implications are.)

———

So moving forward again, I accepted one of the management traineeships I'd been offered, worked for a year as a trainee market researcher and, despite stellar career prospects and lots of money, I was very unhappy. I dreaded going to work, didn't enjoy talking with my colleagues, couldn't relate to the company's values and just felt out of place. I was miserable and knew I was in the wrong environment. Yet at the time, there were very few similar jobs for graduates, and everyone kept telling me how lucky I was to have such a good career and to be making so much money. The thought of staying there though, even for the next few years, made me feel like I was being buried alive.

You could say that the situation created an internal call to adventure in me. And while I hadn't chosen to follow the exciting external call to adventure presented by my California scholarship a few years earlier, I now felt that I had to follow this internal invitation to change in order to save my own life.

So I resigned my job, applied to do an MA in English Literature in the USA, and got a teaching assistantship at the University of Connecticut to pay for my studies. The difference in the way I felt was extraordinary: I loved teaching, loved learning about American literature, enjoyed exploring New England and woke up excited and happy and full of energy every single day. That first autumn in Connecticut felt sensational. I had never before felt so gloriously alive, so aware of all the beautiful colours in nature and of how many ways there were to have fun. I loved my new life and work so much that I ended up doing a PhD in literature at Emory University in Georgia, in a teaching and research career as an English professor and I stayed in America for several years.

My next big call to adventure was triggered by a depression. While loving my work, I was feeling increasingly unhappy in my personal relationship at the time – bored, claustrophobic, disconnected, lonely. At the same time, I was feeling a desire to learn more about personal development, to go on courses, to read, to take workshops with people with similar interests. I tried to ignore how I was feeling and just carried on, perhaps going to the gym too much to distract myself. One day, I fainted and ended up in hospital. I was diagnosed with chronic fatigue syndrome and it took a few months of complete rest to recover. At the same time, I was still feeling very down and wasn't exactly sure why.

Looking back, I can see that my problems were caused by ignoring my initially subtle, yet increasingly intense feelings that something wasn't quite right – that I needed to leave my relationship and to invest more time and energy into understanding myself, what mattered to me, what kind of relationship I really wanted and what direction I wanted to take with my life. Once I got the courage together to leave the relationship and start exploring those things, my energy and moods began to rise and life opened up for me again.

My next invitation to do something exciting, different, enticing and scary came about twelve years ago. My son had recently been born, I had moved back to the UK and got married a few years previously, and I was teaching at an English university. I found that I was enjoying teaching much less than I had in America, where I had felt genuinely delighted each day to share fascinating works of literature with my students, thrilled by the lively intellectual dynamics, the collegiality with other professors and the interesting research and writing I was doing. I was now giving many more lectures to large groups of students and fewer tutorials and small seminars, and although my work still had many positive aspects, I simply wasn't enjoying it the way I used to. Walking back from university one day, I caught myself daydreaming about what other professions/careers could be more stimulating. I had published academic books, received wonderful evaluations from my students, but now felt ready for new challenges, new learning, new opportunities. I knew I wanted to work with people in a way that would inspire them and help them to develop, but I was feeling drawn to focus more on their life and their work; I was attracted to the idea of helping people become happier and more fulfilled. The question was: how?

———

Having invested so many years in my PhD and my academic career, I couldn't imagine what other appealing options might exist. And how could I abandon a career in which I had been so successful and had spent so many years pursuing? And what about leaving a secure financial position for one of uncertainty? It would have been very much easier to have remained a university professor for the next thirty years, occasionally wondering wistfully what else I might have done. However, I didn't do that, as you know!

I read about the new profession of life coaching in *The Times* one day, and felt irresistibly drawn to it. My mind was racing so fast as I reflected on the article, that I couldn't sleep properly for several nights. This was a real, old-fashioned, vocational call – a call to adventure that was completely unmistakable. I registered for an exploratory call with Coach U, the leading coach training institution, loved what I learned and decided to leave teaching and start a two-year course to become a qualified coach.

I'd taken a real leap of faith. As you might imagine, my family and friends all thought that I had gone completely crazy, to be leaving a prestigious, secure, enjoyable job for a career nobody had even heard of at the time. (Was I going to be a lifeguard, someone asked!) I remember comments like, 'It's so American! English people would never want to work with a coach!' In fact, I heard endless discouraging comments along those lines. There was also the very

---

compelling and scary point that with senior academic jobs in English Literature in London being so very rare, it was likely that if I left this position, I would find it almost impossible to rejoin the profession.

Nevertheless, I felt I knew what I had to do, and I took the big leap, doing whatever it took to finish my training and build my coaching business in a climate where nobody understood what it actually was. In my first year of coaching, I was getting steady referrals from happy clients, and was increasingly confident that I would be able to generate a comfortable living from my new business. Since then, I've absolutely loved every aspect of my career – making a difference to people, enjoying the way coaching draws on my strengths and reflects my values and fascinated by the constant learning with every new client, every new company I work with. Looking back, I am so happy and pleased that I had the courage to leave university teaching and follow my call towards being a coach.

Personally, as well as professionally, my life so far has involved significant change, including getting divorced several years ago, experiencing a wonderfully happy relationship for many years after that and, recently, becoming single again. If I hadn't taken the decision to leave my marriage, I wouldn't have the amazing life I do today. Most mornings I wake up feeling really joyful about the day ahead.

BACK TO YOU

But enough stories! Let's get back to you and why you're reading this book.

I shared my story simply to show you that I myself have had several calls to adventures, personally and professionally, some of which I've followed and some of which I haven't. Having had such an eventful life so far, I'm able to draw on my own experiences of dramatic change to understand and support my coaching clients, and the challenges, opportunities, and life-defining choices they face. Having made so many changes myself, and achieved, as a consequence, my own extremely fulfilling work and life, I have confidence that (almost) anything is possible for people if they are clear and focused and purposeful in their pursuit of it.

WHAT HAPPENS IF YOU TURN DOWN OR IGNORE THE CALL?

We always have the choice to turn down the call or to put energy into ignoring it. But this is dangerous. It can feel safer not to go on the adventure, but paradoxically it's not.

Calls to adventure are stubborn things, and they keep reappearing until it's impossible to ignore them, or they reappear in different forms – a bit like my decision to go to the States after turning down the California scholarship earlier.

If we resolutely refuse opportunities, we can eventually feel regretful, haunted by the opening doors we have chosen not to walk through, as T. S. Eliot expresses in *Four Quartets* ('Burnt Norton', pt I):

> Footfalls echo in the memory
> Down the passage which we did not take
> Towards the door we never opened
> Into the rose-garden.

Rather than expanding into greater possibilities and happiness, instead we can start to contract and close down, get more rigid, more predictable, less open to the new, the spontaneous, the undiscovered.

If at midlife, defined broadly as mid-thirties to mid-fifties, we have the opportunity to grow, the chance for individuation, we also have the much scarier risk of closing down and getting stuck. What's the opposite of individuation? I see it as settling down in the worst sense, rather than growing up – this is important. What happens if you ignore the internal call and just distract yourself?

———

You end up preoccupied with externals, focused on material gain and materialism, watching too much TV, focusing on your appearance, eating and/or drinking too much, playing too many computer games – essentially choosing to numb yourself with superficial external apparent fixes. You can avoid growing up by running from relationship to relationship, trying to find that external fix, when really the only place to find it is by understanding what's true for you more deeply and then making your life reflect that truth.

You can respond to the call to change with negativity and pessimism, just focusing on what's lost, rather than being grateful for what you have and for what's possible and real and just out there for you around the next corner. You can distract yourself with mind- and body-numbing pursuits that kill time and energy, or you can put one foot in front of the other in a purposeful way, determined to uncover what's possible for you.

T. S. Eliot writes in the *Four Quartets* about returning to where you started in your journey, but returning renewed and different, and finding the place therefore changed. Sometimes, it's not about making dramatic changes in the externals of your life, but more subtle personal growth and development which ends up renewing everything for you and those closest to you, creating a situation where you return to your beginning, but return transformed.

———

WHAT HAPPENS IF YOU FOLLOW THE CALL?

If you consciously decide to accept the call to adventure, to go on your particular quest, however the quest makes itself known to you in the unique circumstance of your own life, you make it possible to define what constitutes treasure for you, your dream destination, find it and bring it back into your everyday experience moving forward. It's a choice you make for yourself – and one you make bravely, consciously, deliberately. Only you will know what your particular quest looks like and what might be on the other side of possibility for you if you go for it.

It's not about walking on hot coals and getting a pep talk about your extraordinary powers. It's not about changing your life in a weekend. It's not about an instant breakthrough of any kind, in fact. And it's not about taking a grown-up gap year to travel the world and 'find yourself', however glamorous and appealing that might sound.

It's altogether more mundane, more practical, and yet, paradoxically, more exciting and illuminating too. It's about becoming more soulful, more purposeful, finding the work, the relationship, the lifestyle that is most suited to your unique self.

It's finding and enjoying soulful love, whatever that

---

means for you. It's about doing work you love – work that you look forward to, and that actively thrills you. It's about understanding how to be your absolute best and how to be happiest, and then living a life that reflects that every day.

And the amazing thing about the challenge and call to adventure is that it provides the catalyst for you to start changing your life today in order to reach your dream destination, starting right this minute with your intention to create that for yourself.

I want nothing less for you, because it really is possible; and with the right clarity, plan and follow-through, you can do it. I absolutely know this from working with so many clients who have achieved it, and from what I've achieved in my own life.

LET'S GO!

Just as you wouldn't set out on a real-life journey without the kit you need to be prepared, safe and have fun along the way, you need to be prepared for this journey too. And I will be by your side as you go.

This book will show you how you can help yourself to understand who you want to be and where you're headed – to find your way through Dante's 'dark wood' (see p. 2), to give you the practical tools you'll require, and whatever else you need on your journey to ensure that you're prepared and ready to come out with your treasure as you emerge into the light of your dream destination.

Let's get started!

CHAPTER 2

From Here to There (or There to Here)

In the first chapter, we looked at those disorientating wake-up moments in our lives, those jolts out of our comfort zone – the points at which you realise that anything that doesn't make you feel alive is simply not right for you. We considered what a call to adventure is and what it feels like, the opportunities and challenges presented by change. And I made the point that it's often just when things appear to be falling apart that something magical may be about to happen if we can see the situation with hope.

In this chapter, we're going to turn our attention to the journey itself and its context. If something external happens to you that shakes your world, like losing your job,

---

how do you travel from that point of confusion to somewhere wonderful, somewhere where you have a fulfilling job you love? If you know from the inside out that something or everything has to change for you to be happy, how do you create a clear sense of what specifically you're aiming for, and how do you chart a road map? What is your dream destination, in fact?

What's at stake? What should you expect on the road from here to there? What might get in the way of your success? What can you do about it? And what tools, skills, approaches, and knowledge do you need to succeed in your quest? In this chapter we will address all these questions and I will explain how creating a Personal Vision Day can be a brilliant and inspiring launch pad to help you find your calling and identify the path that will lead to your happiness and fulfilment. Ready?

Let's start by looking at what you are aiming for. The first thing to emphasise is that you need to expand your sense of what's possible, to be more ambitious for yourself and your life. Let's look at some specific examples at different life stages.

In your twenties, you might be trying hard to get your career on track, or maybe even struggling to decide what track is the right one for you. You may not be in a relationship with the person you want to spend your life with yet, and be beginning to wonder if it's ever going to happen.

In your thirties, you might be building your career at the same time as you're starting your family, trying to juggle your relationship and the demands of being a parent with your work. Perhaps you're trying to include fun in the picture too, and finding it increasingly hard. Or you might well still be searching for that elusive special someone.

In your forties, you might find that you're questioning where you are in work and life and how you got there. Is your career your real calling? Is your relationship making you happy? Perhaps you're going through a difficult divorce. Are all the various pieces in your life fitting together in a way that really works for you, or are there some adjustments and recalibrations you need to make?

In your fifties, you might be dealing with teenagers at the same time as ageing parents. Perhaps you're considering starting your own business, changing your work pattern to free up more play time, recharging your vitality by learning something new, maybe buying a house abroad where you can decamp during the winters.

But whether you're choosing to alter your life or whether you have changes, possibly big ones, forced upon you, any change can be wonderful and exciting or unsettling and scary. Most usually, it's a mixture.

What if you could use the specific presenting issue that launches you on the path to change as a magical catalyst to get you into another world? What if what seems to be

---

a terrible problem is actually a wonderful opportunity? What about Alice, falling down the rabbit hole, drinking the potion that makes her small? It may seem like a catastrophe at first glance, but it means she can enter the enchanted garden. How does the picture change if we go from wondering how we can get through the day/week/month/Christmas to asking ourselves how we can find a way to be genuinely joyful?

Ultimately, when something seems difficult, it's our attitude that will determine a successful outcome. Rather than looking for a way out, we need to look for a way. And it starts by living in the present; it starts with your day today, with a single step ...

DO YOU KNOW WHERE YOU'RE GOING TO? (AND WHY YOU WANT TO GO THERE)

One of the secrets to getting what you want is actually knowing what you want. It may sound obvious, but a surprisingly large number of us aren't sure about what we want, which then makes the journey of getting it much harder than it needs to be. If a genie mysteriously appeared in your living room this evening and asked you what your three wishes were, would you know how to answer? In children's fairy stories, the plot often revolves around wishes going dramatically wrong, because they are not sufficiently specific or thought out.

You may have heard of the law of attraction, of cosmic ordering, and *The Secret* – either the book by Rhonda Byrne or the film based upon the book. Whether or not you are comfortable with the possible over-simplification of these principles, as a coach I can tell you with confidence that one of the keys to my clients' success is helping them to become crystal clear about what exactly they want to achieve. They often come to me having tried to achieve particular goals for years with little success. The real secret lies in making sure that the goals you choose are really the right ones for the unique individual you are. That, and getting inspired to the point where you can expand your thinking so that you can really stretch to achieve something compelling and real. For example, rather than just thinking you want to get another job, why not take the opportunity to find an extremely fulfilling job, even a thrilling one, perhaps in an area you hadn't considered before? Or, rather than just bemoaning the fact that you can't lose those last stubborn seven pounds, why not create a project to make yourself gorgeous? Something that would encompass losing those extra pounds, but would be much more interesting and satisfying than a straightforward diet, and fun too! If

---

you can enjoy the path towards reaching your goals, your chances of success are significantly higher than if you approach it with an attitude of grimly determined self-denial.

Your Personal Vision Day will help you to clarify your goals, and we'll be looking at this later in the chapter. For now, though, let me share with you some landmarks that form a part of everyone's dream destination – objectives that I help all my coaching clients to achieve, whatever the details of their goals. Ultimately, I believe that under the surface of daily busy-ness, we all want to be our best, to understand and express ourselves more fully in the world, to use our full range of gifts to their utmost potential. We want to feel healthy, vital, energised, to wake up each morning feeling excited about the day ahead of us. We want our relationships and work to live up to our aspirations. We want to know where we're going, to know what our purpose in life is. We want to know what our calling is and to follow it. We may not explicitly articulate this or even consciously realise it, but underneath the surface stream, that's what's true. More basically, we want to have fun, be happy, feel able to live in the moment and thoroughly enjoy the present, rather than wasting our lives trapped in the past or dreaming about the future.

Whatever particular situation, challenge or opportunity brings my clients to me for that first conversation, I always find that these are the results they're really after, even if they don't express them to me in so many words. And it's achieving these results that make them so satisfied and happy at the end of the coaching process; not just to have met particular goals, but to have learned how to be their best selves. And what a practical difference it makes, to get self-mastery and the skills and awareness to make the most of each moment, while thoroughly enjoying the moment too and feeling grateful, peaceful, even joyful. I can tell you that you can achieve all this for yourself.

Creating a big-picture vision of how you want your life to unfold is more powerful and compelling than just listing a number of unconnected goals. When we start to work on your vision, it must be one that will excite you, make your heart beat faster, stretch you and pull you into your future.

It's also important to remember that it's not just your ideal destination that matters, it's also the journey itself that counts – how you enjoy and appreciate every step along the way that takes you where you want to go. It's as much about the yellow-brick road as it is about Oz. For example, think about doing an amazingly choreographed beautiful dance, perhaps a challenging cha cha cha, a joyful jive or a terrific tango. The objective isn't just to get through to the end of the dance as quickly as possible, but to enjoy every step along the way – to hear the music, feel the rhythm of the dance, take pleasure in each lovely

———

moment as it leads naturally into the next step. With that in mind, let me invite you to take a ten-minute break.

TAKE A TEN-MINUTE BREAK FOR REFLECTION
(YES, RIGHT NOW)

If you're reading at home, why not make a cup of tea, go and sit in the garden and enjoy the flowers and the birds? Or have a glass of wine, light the fire and sit reflectively for ten minutes, listening to your favourite music. If you're on a train, take a few minutes to look out of the window and admire the sun rising, setting or shining. What can you do in this very moment to think a happy or inspiring thought, consider what you're grateful for, reflect on something that makes you smile? If you're commuting home, why not pick up some dazzling flowers to light up your bedroom at the beginning and end of each day?

WHAT TO EXPECT ON THE JOURNEY

Let's assume that you now understand how you can view your own particular challenge or desire to move forward as a call to adventure; you've got a sense that you might, in fact, be able to turn this apparent obstacle into something amazing for yourself, and you understand that moving from where you are to who and where you want to be is going to mean embarking on a journey. Let's call it your hero's or heroine's journey, because it is exactly that. You are the hero or heroine of your own life and you're getting ready to go on a quest to discover some fabulous treasure for yourself – treasure that you can use to enrich and transform your life.

On this journey of yours, there are several stages and it's helpful for you to understand them and recognise them in advance, so that you don't allow yourself to get blocked or stuck when you encounter them in real life. If you understand where you are in the process of change, and what's normal, you can gently encourage yourself forward at points that might otherwise feel like blocks.

If you are in the situation of having change forced upon you, perhaps losing something that seemed like a permanent part of your life, then you might well be somewhere along what Elisabeth Kübler-Ross calls the five stages of grief. These are denial, anger, bargaining, depression and acceptance. If you've suffered a bereavement, for example, you are very likely to travel through those stages in your own way at your own pace, and could perhaps benefit from counselling to come to terms with your loss. If the change is something traumatic, but not on quite the same scale, such as divorce or job loss, you will probably still need to travel through these stages, but can positively encourage yourself forward, so that you reach acceptance as soon as possible and don't get stuck in anger or depression.

As soon as you can get yourself into the positively receptive state of acceptance, you can move forward to transform your situation and feel better.

To illustrate my point, let me describe a funny cartoon to you. It's entitled 'The Five Stages of Recession' by Tom Fishburne and it uses the stages of grief as a metaphor for the stages of recession. It comprises five mini-pictures:

- The first shows Denial: it's raining, and a man is saying, hopefully: 'It will be a quick recovery.'

- The second shows Anger: it's still raining, the water is rising and the man is shaking a fist at the sky, complaining, 'My plans are ruined'.

- The third picture depicts Bargaining: it's still raining, the water is rising further, and the man is on his knees in the water, asking, 'How the heck am I supposed to do more with less?'

- The fourth picture represents Depression: the water is up to the man's chest, he looks as if he's battling overwhelm and the caption reads, 'Keep calm and carry on'.

- Things take a turn for the better in the fifth picture which represents Acceptance. It's still raining, the water is covering almost the entire picture, but the man is snorkelling in a multi-coloured sea (the other pictures were black and white). In this last picture we can see a humorous representation of how apparent adversity can be turned into an opportunity, if we progress through the stages of grief and adapt ourselves to the new environment.

Thinking about your own situation, if you have faced (or are facing) a painful change that has been forced upon you, ask yourself if you are progressing through the stages, and what kind of support you might need to move forward to acceptance. Are you blocked somewhere and how can you recognise this? Are you able and willing to encourage yourself forward with a positive mindset and the help of this book?

If, on the other hand, you have decided yourself to initiate positive change in your life and make something wonderful happen, you are probably already at the snorkelling stage and ready to find the technicolour sea to swim in.

In terms of what to expect on the journey, the first and most obvious thing is to recognise that your call to adventure may be surprising or slightly scary, but that if it resonates with you, appeals to you and draws you forward, follow the call and don't be tempted to refuse it, even if

------

you're apprehensive. You may be inclined to resist change, to stay stuck in denial or/and anger, or even bargaining and depression; you may be covering your ears, afraid even to listen to the invitation to the journey.

I find sometimes with new clients that they have been wanting to make changes in their lives and work for some time, but have been putting it off through fear of getting started. Fear of the unknown and fear of change are probably the most common reasons for refusing the call to adventure in the first place.

Fear of failure can also hold you back, whether or not you are consciously aware of it. You may have a cherished dream you think about from time to time, something that inspires you and makes you feel happy and comforted. Perhaps you are afraid, again consciously or not, that if you do go for it, you might fail and then be left with nothing. This fear is worth facing head on, as, realistically, if you don't go for it, and take deliberate steps to turn your dreams into reality, the reality is that you will never achieve your dreams. You need to be brave enough to take one step forward at a time, knowing that not trying will create certain failure, and that even if you don't get to the moon, you may well reach some stars.

You may find that other people in your life don't want you to change, that they feel a bit threatened by the prospect of you developing. You might even face opposition from them, along the lines of, 'Why do you want to lose weight? You're fine the way you are,' for example. At these challenging moments, it's key to hold on to your conviction and your clarity, and not to let yourself be discouraged or diverted. Remember why you decided to make the change in the first place. You might find it helpful to write down all the reasons why making this particular change is important to you, so that you have something to refer back to in those wobbly moments. For example, how will you feel when you have achieved your goal? What will it mean to you? Why is the change worth making? What difference will it make to your life?

WHAT MIGHT GET IN THE WAY (AND WHAT TO DO ABOUT IT)

Assuming that you have decided to follow your call to adventure, that you've embarked on your exciting journey of change, you may still (probably will) face potential roadblocks along the way that could stop you in your tracks. Think, for example, about *The Hobbit*, and how Bilbo Baggins is challenged by various obstacles – trolls, poisonous spiders, the frightening Mirkwood – as he ventures towards the dragon's treasure. Or the reality TV show, *I'm A Celebrity, Get Me Out of Here*, in which contestants face, if not trolls, actual terrors like real spiders, assorted creepy-crawlies, heights, water, not to mention the challenge of living in close proximity to their fellow adventurers. Or the challenges posed by Lord Sugar to the young hopefuls in *The Apprentice*. I believe that these popular TV shows appeal to us because they give us the opportunity to experience adventure vicariously, at second-hand, to share in other people's visible journeys of growth and development and feel inspired by them.

As you probably already know, being prepared is a crucial ingredient in success. If you know what to expect, you can be prepared, and have strategies in place for potential pitfalls. Equally, you will know what's normal and when you should just keep calm and carry on. A book called *What To Expect When You're Expecting* was the pregnancy bible when I was expecting my first child; I remember how reassuring it was as a pregnancy novice to read about the normal, predictable stages my body and emotions would go through over the next several months.

We've already mentioned the normal stages of loss and grief which can catalyse your journey or potentially stop you in your tracks. Equally, any hero's journey contains predictable challenges, dangers and possibilities. Earlier, we discussed how fear can stop you from following your call to

---

adventure – can, in fact, stop the journey before it properly starts.

Assuming that you are ready to embark on your journey, what challenges should you be prepared for?

Self-esteem issues

One thing to watch out for is low self-esteem, self-doubt and self-questioning. It's always surprising to me how many coaching clients, at some point and in some way, voice the question of whether they really deserve to be outrageously happy, whether or not it's self-indulgent to focus on identifying and achieving their dreams.

Once you choose to cultivate your self-belief, you make your journey to change much more likely to succeed, and much more fun too. It's crucial to believe that you are and can be amazing – to believe in your brilliance, your worth and your potential. My coaching company's motto is: 'Shine! Illuminate Your Life'. I chose this line because I find it thrilling on a daily basis to see how my coaching clients can bring out their best and achieve things they wouldn't have believed possible. And yet all they are doing, ultimately, is giving themselves permission to be their unique, brilliant, best selves. Marianne Williamson, leading spiritual author of books including, *A Return To Love: Reflections on the Principles of a Course in Miracles*, has written eloquently about why it's important to let yourself shine:

> We ask ourselves, Who am I to be brilliant, gorgeous, talented, fabulous? Actually, who are you not to be? You are a child of God. Your playing small does not serve the world. There is nothing enlightened about shrinking so that other people won't feel insecure around you. We are all meant to shine, as children do. We were born to make manifest the glory of God that is within us. It's not just in some of us; it's in everyone. And as we let our own light shine, we unconsciously give other people permission to do the same. As we are liberated from our own fear, our presence automatically liberates others.

In other words, as you free yourself to become your best self and live accordingly, you become a charismatic example to others, helping them to free themselves and follow your example.

Self-talk

As long as you are consciously aware of the messages you're giving yourself, the internal dialogue you're having, you have the ability to rescript what you're saying and turn it into something positive and encouraging. All too often, however, people tend to play a negative tape of messages and thoughts in their heads which is very self-destructive; and perhaps the worst aspect of this is that they are not consciously aware of how they're basically hypnotising themselves into staying small, trapped and blue.

So one of the most important things you can do to help yourself successfully deal with change is to practise positive self-talk. For many people, learning to rescript their internal dialogue and talk to themselves helpfully, supportively, and constructively means learning something new. Whenever you learn something new, there are four stages:

1. **Unconscious incompetence**, when you're doing something wrong and you don't know what you don't know – for example if you don't know how to drive a car, but you don't yet know what's even involved in driving; here, you may be telling yourself you're a hopeless loser and why bother to try to change, but you may not be consciously aware that you're giving yourself these messages.

2. **Conscious incompetence**, when you're doing something wrong, but you're aware of it – for example, if you don't know how to drive, but you've had a lesson or two, and you understand all the things you're

doing wrong; here you're telling yourself the same thing as in the example above, but at least you're aware of it.

3. **Conscious competence**, when you're doing something right, but you have to consciously concentrate in order to do it correctly – for example, if you're a new driver and you have your licence, but you still need to think about what you're doing; you might be telling yourself, when you remember to do so, that you're bright and have achieved things in the past and can do so again.

4. **Unconscious competence**, when you can do something correctly and you're so comfortable doing it that you don't even have to think about it – for example, you're a confident driver, and you can drive almost automatically, and you can listen to music and carry on a conversation while you're driving. Here, you will naturally be giving yourself positive, inspiring, reassuring messages without thinking about it.

The important point here is to realise that whenever you're learning something new, you have to be patient with yourself and consciously practise the new skill long enough for it to become a natural habit. I find that people often feel that as soon as they reach conscious competence, i.e. they know what they should be doing and they can do it if they consciously try, that they shouldn't have to put more time and effort into it, and that it should happen naturally. Typically it will, but only after sustained practice.

With self-talk, the most insidious, sabotaging point is when you're playing a negative tape in your head, with words like, 'I'm not good enough', 'Who am I kidding?', 'I'll never be able to do that' – but you are not consciously aware of how you are draining your energy. As soon as you are conscious of what you're saying to yourself, even if you're still saying it, you've progressed one learning stage to conscious incompetence, which is actually a huge leap. Because now that your negative self-talk is conscious, you have the ability to turn it around, and, with deliberate, sustained effort, you can create some positive, encouraging, affirming messages for yourself.

So always, and especially before you start an exciting life journey, remember to rescript your self-talk – what you say to yourself about yourself, the messages you give yourself – making sure that you are encouraging, positive, supportive and understanding. Think about how you would speak to your best friend if he or she was doing something new, challenging, exciting and maybe a bit scary. We often speak to ourselves much more judgmentally and critically than we would speak to someone we love. So be aware of this, and if you're discouraging yourself, at least make sure

———

73

you're consciously incompetent, so that you can ramp up a level to conscious competence.

Self-sabotage

Along similar lines, something else that can trip you up on your journey from here to there is self-sabotage. For example, if you've committed to going to the gym Tuesday and Thursday evenings, so that you can become fitter and more energised, if you skip lunch on Tuesday, you'll probably be too exhausted by the end of the day to contemplate a workout. Or if you've set aside Saturday morning for an inspiring visioning time, just you, your journal, music and coffee, don't have such a late night on Friday that you end up sleeping in until lunchtime.

The ways in which we can self-sabotage are, unfortunately, endless, but the main thing is to work out what you need to do for yourself positively to honour your commitments to your own happiness and development, and make sure to make it happen, rather than making excuses.

I've noticed in my many years of coaching that it's often just before a major breakthrough, that you will suddenly find yourself facing resistance. It's something like the darkness-before-the-dawn cliché, and yet I definitely see a similar recurring pattern: typically, right before someone is about to achieve what they've dreamed of and strived for, they do something self-sabotaging.

For example, I'm working with a client at the moment to help her find her ideal work and vocation. Ann has been a stay-at-home mother for some years and one child has now left home, while the other is heading in that direction. She feels rather lost and aimless, and wants to find work that inspires her and gives a focus and purpose to her life, rather than filling her time with coffee mornings and French classes. We've been working through a process for several months now, identifying all the various little and large energy drains, and, where possible, clearing them up one at a time in order to raise her energy, understanding her personality, needs, values and strengths, and coming up with a list of criteria for her ideal work and possible work areas. Last week, we created a top ten of potentially perfect work areas, and I invited her to research a couple of them before our next coaching meeting, even to do a day's volunteer work in two of them to find out first-hand what it would be like to work in those environments.

Perhaps not surprisingly, given the breakthrough/ resistance pattern outlined above, I received a panicky email from Ann after our last coaching meeting, saying she'd become suddenly anxious about the work questions and investigations and thought that maybe she should just go back to teaching yoga part-time, something she qualified for years ago, but had discounted as a serious way forward for work.

Why does resistance before breakthrough happen, do you think? I wonder if it's fear of success, fear of happiness, fear of really living our best life and being our best self. The good news, though, is that if you're aware you might suddenly feel very resistant to moving forward, just when you're on the verge of achieving what you want, be brave and keep progressing, and don't allow yourself to self-sabotage. By being aware ahead of time that you might suddenly notice resistance or sabotage when you're close to success, you will be prepared for it when it happens. And being prepared should allow you to keep going and prevent you from being derailed. Notice the scared feelings or self-sabotaging thoughts you might be experiencing at these moments. Take some deep breaths, recognise the thoughts and feelings for what they really are, reassure yourself and keep moving steadily forward.

WHAT YOU NEED TO SUCCEED

Now that we've looked at what might block you from turning challenge into opportunity, let's spend a little time looking at how you can maximise your chances of success.

Just to remind you that in Part 2, 'Getting Where You Want to Go' (see p. 95), I will be sharing with you a step-by-step action plan to create a road map for your individual journey. What I'm inviting you to do now is to prepare for your adventure, consider what you need to be aware of and create a clear framework of understanding for what you're about to do as you embark on your journey. Here's your top ten (well, eleven actually) things to do to get ready.

Getting mentally inspired

1. **Let go of limiting beliefs and thoughts which don't support you.** Think about your thoughts as the furniture of your mind. Make sure your thoughts are positive and affirming. As I mentioned earlier, pay attention to the messages you're giving yourself. You want to surround yourself with beautiful, inspiring, comfortable furniture in your mental landscape, so that you feel comfortable and uplifted each time you think about your challenges, your opportunities, your journey and what you're trying to create for yourself.

2. **Make sure you're focused on moving from the present to the future**, not going back to the past. When you're creating your future, think about forming it from dreams of what you want your future to be, not

from what didn't work in the past. In other words, create your future from your future, not your past. In a sense, what is being asked of you is to become a master/mistress of two worlds, simultaneously keeping awareness of who you were in the past and who you might become in the future.

3. **Focus on the beautiful, the positive** – the things in your life you appreciate and are grateful for. To a large extent, what you see ahead of you is defined by what you expect to see. As the poet William Blake wrote: 'If the lens of perception is cleansed, everything would appear as it is, infinite.' So try to see the possible, the good, the opportunity, the blessing in each moment and day. Proust puts it like this: 'The real voyage of discovery consists not in seeking new landscapes, but in having new eyes.'

4. **Expand your thinking**. I often find with my coaching clients that the goals they set for themselves at the beginning of our coaching relationship are far smaller and less exciting than what they are capable of achieving and what they do, in fact, usually achieve. For example, a client might come to me and say they want a promotion, to lose ten pounds and to have a more harmonious personal relationship. But with work, focus and inspiration they may get a huge

promotion and pay rise, or break away and start their own successful business; they may well get in the best physical shape they've ever been, whatever their age, and feel totally delighted by how they feel and look physically; and rather than just having a more harmonious personal relationship, they may fall back in love with their partner and feel re-inspired about their life together.

5. **Embrace who you are and your own uniqueness**. Your path to brilliant success lies in becoming *your* best self, not a mediocre version of someone else. Later in the book, we're going to explore how to understand – really understand in depth – who you are, what makes you happy and who you have the potential to be/what your best self looks like. Dr Seuss has a catchy way of reminding us of what's important: 'Today You are You. It is truer than true. There is no one alive who is Youer than You.' In order to build a fabulous life of your own, don't waste your time measuring yourself against others.

6. **Be patient**. I often tell my clients that growth and development are like spirals rather than a linear line. Sometimes, you will appear to be back where you were, but almost always you'll find the similarity is deceptive as your perspective is enhanced and more

sophisticated. You're simply revisiting a familiar area from a different level. Growth takes time. And there is no greater investment than investing in yourself. It's better to invest quality time in quality development, so that at the end of each particular journey, you have the tools to make the positive changes sustainable. In my coaching programmes, I invite my clients to commit to working together for a year, as it takes that long, in my experience, to create really sustainable changes. Not that you can't make all kinds of exciting changes along the way, because you can and will.

Getting physically inspired

7. **You'll need reserves of physical energy and vitality** for your exciting journey towards positive change. Practically, that means getting physically fit and feeling good about yourself physically. You need to get enough sleep to feel thoroughly rested, do enough exercise (and the right kind for you) to energise and uplift you and eat a healthy, delicious diet to make you feel your best. It's a good idea to focus on physical health and vitality before you start your journey, or if not before you start, then certainly throughout and especially during the first three months. Energy is fundamentally important. It's easy to take our bodies

and physical health for granted, live in our heads and get used to feeling 60 per cent physically, rather than 95 per cent, say. And the difference between what you can do and who you can be at 60 per cent vs 95 per cent is huge! So pay attention to this area and make an action plan for yourself. When you have felt your absolute healthy, glowing best, what were you eating and what was your exercise pattern? What is your own particular recipe for feeling your absolute best? Write down a plan for yourself and check in with it regularly to note the results and your progress.

Getting emotionally and spiritually inspired

8. **Self-care**. I encourage my clients to practise extreme self-care. What does this mean? It means looking after yourself so that you can build reserves of time, energy and the feelgood factor. You can then draw on these reserves to make amazing things happen for yourself. More about this later in the book, but for now, just think about what you need to do to really look after yourself and get energised. I invite my clients to make a list of things they can do every day that make them happy. Examples include sitting for 10 minutes somewhere beautiful in nature or going for a walk and enjoying the scenery, playing with your children,

having a proper, connected chat with your partner or a friend, keeping fresh flowers in your house . . .

9. **Rally emotional support for your journey** from here to there, from good to great. Identify family, friends and colleagues to cheer you on, people who believe in you and who will be unconditionally constructive. I've known clients who've thrown a 'New Me' party to which they've invited their unofficial team of supporters and asked for their help and encouragement, with a promise to invite them to their celebration party once they've reached their dream destination (or milestones along the way). You might consider joining a coaching group or working individually with a coach (I recommend you choose a professionally certified coach, see Resources, p. 235, if you decide on the latter route).

10. **Celebrate!** Not just at the end of your journey, but at every milestone reached along the way from here to there. It's really important to acknowledge yourself for every small step. We will work later on identifying milestones along your path through the metaphorical forest. Each time you achieve something, make sure you give yourself a huge pat on the back and contact someone in your support network to celebrate with you, even if it's just a coffee out or a celebratory walk somewhere beautiful.

---

11. **Make a strong emotional connection with your goals**. Later on, we will work on making sure that the goals you choose are the right ones for you. You need to feel passionately committed to them in order to move forward and achieve them. And your passion to achieve them needs to be greater than the moments of fear which will try to block you. So do what you need to do to get in touch with your excitement about your dream destination, so that this feeling propels you forward through any obstacles that might appear in your path. This might involve giving yourself a pep talk, reminding yourself why you want to achieve your goals or make those changes or perhaps writing in your journal or talking to a positive friend. You need to find that vital element which is big enough for you and discover what you feel called to achieve, what will make you feel most truly alive.

YOUR VISION DAY (PART ONE)

As you read through Part 2 of this book, 'Getting Where You Want to Go', you will read about the steps to take and the tools to use to make your journey fun and successful.

Before you get started on the actual journey though, you'll need to decide where you want to go! What is your dream destination? And that's where your first Vision Day comes in.

What is a Vision Day?

A Vision Day is a day devoted exclusively to creating and defining your vision for yourself – your vision for what you want to achieve in your life and in your work.

I run Vision Days with my coaching clients regularly. They are an incredibly powerful, focusing and effective way to shine a light on what you really want – not what you think you want or what you might have wanted in the past, but what you really want now that you didn't even realise before.

I'm going to invite you to hold two Vision Days as we go on this journey of change together. This first one is about creating a broad picture of what you want to change, transform, achieve and create for yourself. As we move through the practical steps marked out on your road map, your vision may change, adapt and come into clearer focus. In fact, it's almost certainly going to become more compelling and specific. So your second Vision Day will be about creating a more detailed picture of what you want to invite into your life.

Creating Your Vision Day

- **Step 1: choose your day** Here's where the fun starts! The first thing to do is to grab your diary, your calendar, your iPhone or whatever you use to organise your time, and look for the first opportunity to create a clear day just for you. The only rule is this: it must be a complete day with no interruptions or other activities to take away from your focus on your vision.

  For some of you, the perfect day might be a Saturday or Sunday, but if you do choose a weekend day, make sure it's one that you can devote to you – so no grocery shopping, making Sunday lunch or other weekend rituals during your day. Some of you might choose to take a day's holiday off work so you can be out of your normal routine, with nothing to do but focus on your dreams. If you have small children and are home-based, be creative about who you can ask to help out and give you some well-deserved free time for yourself.

  Whatever day you choose, make sure it's completely *your* day, and once you've chosen it, write it in your diary, mark it on your calendar and guard it carefully to make sure it doesn't get colonised or interrupted by anyone else. I can't emphasise strongly enough how important it is to keep it *completely free for you.*

Ideally, choose a Vision Day that is a week or two away from today so that you can get prepared. By clearing a full day for yourself, you are giving yourself the message that you are worth taking yourself seriously and you are honouring yourself. I sometimes give clients a formula for creating high self-esteem which really works: self-care + self-respect = self-esteem. In other words, it's what you actually do to take care of yourself, combined with what you say to yourself – so an action as well as a thought component – that leads to high self-esteem, and giving yourself a Vision Day reflects both aspects.

- **Step 2: prepare for your day** Apart from a day's time and space, you'll need some props. I suggest you create a treasure chest for yourself consisting of blank paper, a notebook or journal, pencils (including coloured), pens, crayons, even paints, if you feel creative. If you decide to create a vision board (see p. 88), you will need an A4 (or larger) piece of white card from a stationery or art supplies shop, some glue and some magazine pictures of images you are drawn to.

Give some thought to what would be the most inspiring environment for your Vision Day. Some people find they are most creative and thoughtful in nature, and so might take themselves off to a park, to some beautiful gardens or for a walk by the river. Others will prefer to be at home where they can be still and uninterrupted. If you decide to be at home, make sure you clear whatever space you're working in, so it's tidy, clean and uncluttered. And it's a good idea to burn some aromatherapy oil, play some inspiring music, make your favourite coffee – whatever will get you in the mood for playful inspiration and visioning. It's your own unique, personal Vision Day, so wherever you choose to hold it, inside or outside, make sure the atmosphere is happy and uplifting, allowing you to think and imagine freely.

- **Step 3: create your vision** Where do you start? In any given moment you are being guided by one of two maps, a vision map of your ideal future or a default map, based on your past. Your job now is to create a clear, compelling magnetic vision map to draw you forward to your ideal future. Make a new vision of your future. Let go of any beliefs and thoughts that don't support it. Almost anything is possible if it's right for you and if you work towards achieving it. Don't limit your thinking by what's been true for you in the past.

As I write this, we're at the end of the year, and next year is beckoning like a beautiful pristine white, snowy expanse, full of possibilities, promise and magic. Really, though, your own new year can start at any point when you decide you're ready to create something new and wonderful for yourself. So regardless of when you read this, you can get ready to create your new year.

So what do you want? What do you *really* want? Imagine your life a year from now. Imagine that three important things have changed from how they are now. Imagine that you are feeling overwhelmingly happy and fulfilled and grateful as a result of these three changes. What are they?

Here are some tips to help you get clearer about your vision:

1. **Create a vision board.** You may enjoy putting together a vision board to provide a pictorial representation of what you want to invite into your life and work. If so, you might want to begin your Vision Day with an hour or ninety minutes of vision board creation.

   Consider the qualities, experiences and feelings you want to be part of your life. What pictures and specific images represent those qualities, experiences and feelings? Try to be as precise as possible. I've seen many vision boards with generic pictures of wealth in them, sometimes in the form of bank notes, dollar signs, diamonds, etc., reflecting a desire to be more prosperous. But it's much more effective to take the time to consider what prosperity means to you. What is the essence, the feeling that you want to achieve? It's probably not money per se, but an experience. And if you choose a picture that really speaks to you and resonates precisely, rather than a generic image, it will work much more magnetically on your vision board. For example, it could be a picture of a holiday that you would really like to have, an image of a gorgeous outfit or a picture of your ideal house by the sea. Choose pictures from magazines and other sources that inspire you and represent the feelings and experiences you want to invite into your life. Then cut the pictures out and stick them on your vision board, creating whatever pattern or shape you feel like.

I've had several uncanny experiences with clients for whom the images on their vision boards materialised almost exactly as they were represented. In all of these cases, they had taken the time, trouble and thought, to think beyond the clichés and generalities to find images that were a more personal and particular representation of what they wanted to attract into their lives. The key is to go for the feeling, the experience you wish to have, not just the object that might seem to represent it.

Once you have your own personal vision board, covered in pictures and images that inspire you and propel you forward, make sure it's somewhere very visible where you can see it and be energised by it every day.

2. **Create a journal.** You might prefer to write a journal to capture your vision, or use a notebook in which to capture your thoughts. Some people find it helpful to buy a beautifully designed leather or cloth notebook, something that is a visual representation of the feelings they want to create. For others, a simple pad is enough.

Whatever you choose to write in or on, you can either write freely or use bullet points for categories such as personal, health, family, fun, etc. If you decide to free-write, I suggest you devote approximately forty-five minutes to writing whatever comes into your head, without stopping and without censoring yourself. You may surprise yourself by what you discover in the course of writing. Either way, I want you to expand your thinking and take a big leap of faith to imagine your biggest, most exciting dream about how you would like your life and work to be. As I mentioned earlier, your vision should pull you into your future, be a stretch to move you forward. Ask yourself questions like: what am I doing? Where am I living? What am I feeling? Who am I with? Writing in the present tense can bring your vision to life.

3. **Create a playlist or paint a picture.** Other ways to explore your vision include creating a playlist where the songs convey the qualities you wish for your own life, or painting a picture.

Be as creative as you want on your Vision Day, and feel free to mix up different approaches. Regardless of what you choose though, at some point during your Vision Day it's helpful to write down the changes that you want to make in your life over the next year. Studies have found that people who write down their goals are much more likely to achieve them, and I've witnessed the same thing many times with my coaching clients. But don't worry if your Vision Day goals are still quite general – more energy, more time with your children, a more fulfilling career, getting fitter, for example – as at this point we're just trying to get a sense of the big picture we're moving towards. Later in the programme, we will create more detailed goals.

But what I would like to invite you to do is to end your Vision Day with a vision for yourself that you're truly inspired by:

———

- Expand your sense of what's possible. For example, describe the changes that you would like to see in your relationship: you would like to spend more time with your partner and have more fun together, perhaps. What would be even better than that? Let's go 25 per cent higher. For example, you might say you also want to go away for fun, romantic weekend trips together every few months, and have one amazing holiday together each year, taking turns to choose the destination. Good. And what could be even better than that? Let's go 25 per cent higher again. What about adding more romance and more passion into the mix. Great. How about if you imagined it even better than that? What would that look like? Let's go 25 per cent higher again. How about all of the above, plus learning new things together, such as salsa dancing or diving? Fantastic! That's a Vision Day result and gives you something to focus on and work towards.

- Create a conscious, deliberate intention that this next year is going to be your best year yet.

- And believe! As Saint Augustine wrote, 'Faith is to believe what we do not see; and the reward of this faith is to see what we believe.'

At the end of your first Vision Day you should have a vision for yourself that you believe in, one you are committed to and feel passionate about. This vision represents your dream destination, the light on the other side of the woods, the forward-propelling force on your journey.

So let's embark on the journey together, with that light shining in front of us. Once we're clearer on who you are at your best and what most inspires you, we will have another Vision Day and make your vision even more compelling and clear. But we're off to a brilliant start for now!

PART 2
GETTING WHERE YOU WANT TO GO

CHAPTER 3

Get Ready to
Enjoy the Journey and
Feel Good Now

Creating a solid foundation of energised wellbeing is by far the best foundation for achieving your goals. If you feel good, you enjoy all your journeys as well as your destinations. You are able to live in the present, rather than delay your happiness to some hypothetical point in the future. Most importantly, you make the journey, your actual experience of living today, as enjoyable and fun as possible.

When my son was smaller, like all children he always wanted to know when he was going to arrive wherever we were going. 'Are we there yet?' 'How long until we get there?' All parents are familiar with this chorus. At the

---

time, I used to sing a song to him: 'We're going to get there when we get there, and have a great time when we do, but half the fun of getting where we're going, is going there with you!' I don't know where the song came from, but it did have the desired effect of lightening the mood, making everyone laugh and reminding the adults in the party of why we were travelling in the first place . . .

People often make the mistake of thinking that achieving their goals will make them feel good. I think it's the other way round, in fact. In my experience with coaching clients to successful results, achieving goals that make you happy (as opposed to goals that may not – an important distinction) is really the consequence of feeling good, balanced and energised. Let me explain.

Have you ever had the experience of striving for particular goals, achieving them and then feeling rather flat about the whole exercise – a 'Now what?' or 'So what?' feeling? All too often, people choose goals that aren't necessarily right for them. These may be goals they'd always assumed they wanted, ideas inherited from their parents, cultural stereotypes, superficial objectives that didn't really speak to them in the first place. When I first speak to new clients and explore with them the goals they have attained so far and how they feel about them, I'm struck by how unusual it is for people to really take the time, energy and thought to contemplate which goals will reflect their personality, express their values, enlist their strengths and make them truly joyful.

If you're not feeling good, happy and positive about your life, you can still achieve goals, but the chances are you won't be in the best frame of mind to set objectives that are really right for you. So even if you achieve them, they may not bring you much joy or even be very satisfying or sustainable. Imagine, for example, a young man in his early twenties. He may leave university feeling unfocused and not really knowing what his vocation is. Perhaps he has a family background of working in finance and, despite his dreams of working in the media, there is pressure on him to follow in his family's footsteps. He decides his goal is to make a lot of money and that the route to that is to become a trader, even though his real passion may lie elsewhere. He may well succeed, and have amassed a fortune by the time he reaches his thirties, but this may have been a joyless, driven exercise, and he may then lose the money almost as quickly as he accumulated it.

On the other hand, if you take valuable time out before you launch yourself along a particular path, consider deeply what your underlying purpose and mission are, who you really are as an individual, what values light you up and inspire you, where your own unique pattern of strengths and values converges, you are far more likely to enjoy the process of moving forward to achieve your goals. If you focus on making yourself happy before and (equally importantly) *during* the goal-setting phase, as well as on the journey forward, you will feel a sense of harmony, flow and ease – a feelgood factor. And feeling clear, balanced, positive, relaxed and energised will mean that the journey is fun, enjoyable and exciting, as well as making it far more likely that you will achieve your goals and arrive at your dream destination.

The initial goals that you came up with in the last chapter (see pp. 55–93) are a valuable starting point, showing you what's possible. But as I've already mentioned, after we have done the work of clearing the energetic decks and decluttering your life, understanding your personality, needs, strengths and values, you're likely to have a far more lucid, expanded perspective and we will then be able to recast your goals to form a revision (re-vision) of your desired destination.

In this chapter, we will focus practically on how to be happy now – to identify and eliminate energy drains, create the momentum to move forward positively and enjoy every step of the journey. Then, in the next chapter we will explore who you really are and what will make you happiest in life. And we will then be ready to set technicolour, ambitious, inspiring goals that are really right for you, and plan how to bring them to fruition.

THE ELUSIVE FEELGOOD FACTOR

Let's start by working out how you (and yes, I do mean *you* individually) can create your own feelgood factor. We want to work out what you need to do so that you can wake up in the morning feeling genuinely happy to be starting a new day of your life, and so you can go to bed at night feeling truly peaceful, centred and grateful for all your blessings in the day that is ending. As I mentioned earlier, this all-important energised state of wellbeing is the magic starting point for defining and achieving your goals.

Because your own individual prescription for feeling good is so personal, the best way to work out its ingredients is to set aside an hour, take a notebook or a blank sheet of paper, sit down somewhere peaceful and inspiring, and articulate and explore what you have done in the past that has made you wake up feeling like it's the beginning of your summer holiday. What is the magic combination of factors that makes you feel good? Is it a combination of physical, mental, emotional and spiritual conditions, or are there particular areas of your experience that have led to you feeling fulfilled? If you don't feel like writing notes to explore this, you may be more drawn to sketching images or perhaps creating a mindmap (p. 102) or diagram with connecting words or pictures.

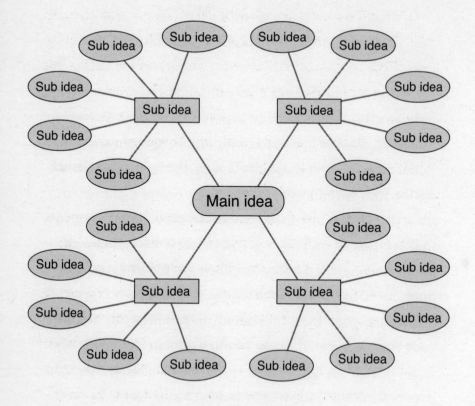

Another way into this is to think about moments in the past when you've felt particularly happy or peaceful. What factors do these moments have in common? For example, as I reflect on these questions myself, what immediately comes to mind are pictures of lunch breaks at school when I was a teenager, lying on the hills that were just above the playground, gazing at the blue sky, watching the clouds moving, feeling the grass under my hands, being immersed in the moment; or being with my childhood sweetheart at school in Rome and then in England; walking on the beach in Florida and collecting seashells; reading bedtime stories to my son, with the cat purring next to us and the sound of the clock ticking; those romantic, connected, timeless moments with my partner, dancing, talking, walking; those transformative points with clients when I see them making break-throughs, being visibly happier ...

Apart from looking at your memorably happy moments thus far, your highlights, it's useful to consider your learn-ing points, the moments when you learn something significant, perhaps change direction or simply change. A revealing exercise is to take an A4 piece of paper and make an outline of your life so far, marking on one page what you've done and where you've been, the highs, the lows, the learning points or 'Aha' moments, the changes of direction. In essence, you're creating a map of your journey thus far, what has led you to this moment, today. Once you've fin-ished sketching this map, I suggest you go and make yourself a cup of tea, take a short walk or perhaps sit out in your garden or on your terrace. When you come back, look at what you have outlined on paper, and ask yourself where you feel moved to direct your journey going forward. Is there a particular place, experience, feeling, colour, desti-nation that calls you forward, that pops into your mind and beckons you enticingly?

———

This exercise can offer you many useful and inspiring clues about how you want your life to unfold going forward, what your most powerful goals might be and what your personal happiness recipe might look like.

But for now, let's put your notes, map, and pictures to one side and look at the very important and practical steps you can take to create your own feelgood factor and, by clearing the decks, get yourself ready to define the goals that are right for the unique individual that you are.

CLEARING YOUR LIFE: ELIMINATING ENERGY DRAINS

One of the first things to do in this journey towards positive change is to energise yourself. Practically speaking, and I do believe in being practical, energising yourself involves identifying all the energy drains in your life and systematically getting rid of as many of them as possible.

Imagine, for example, that your life is represented by a crystal glass and that your energy is represented by spring water inside it. Picture the various energy drains in your life – the things that irritate, worry, upset or even just mildly bother you – as represented by little holes in the glass. Your energy, symbolised by the water, will escape from the glass through these holes. As the water escapes, you will work to re-energise yourself, to fill your glass with more water, more energy, but as fast as you replace it, it leaks out through the holes, through all the various, little let-downs in your life that drain you in various ways. Because of the ways in which your energy escapes every day, your efforts to replace it are only sufficient to maintain the status quo, to keep you in the same place. Your cup doesn't run over with water because of the ongoing loss of energy. And you need your crystal glass or life to be overflowing with water or energy in order to accomplish exciting things, make breakthroughs and move forward in significant ways.

If you think about it, it's a bit pointless to attempt big goals when your energy is being distracted and diverted. Even if you truly want to do exciting things, you won't have the physical, emotional, mental or spiritual resources to do so, unless you minimise energy escape.

In order to raise your energy in a dramatic, yet sustainable way, make a checklist of very basic, practical details in all the main areas of your life that need to be sorted out in order for you to feel your best. I'd suggest you make five or six headings; the following normally work well:

———

- My Home

- My Body

- My Emotional and Mental Wellbeing

- My Money

- My Relationships

- My Work

Under each of these headings, write ten to twelve statements that when ticked make you feel good, or when not checked, make you mildly or significantly irritated or upset. Here is what the list might look like:

My Home:

1. When I walk into my home I feel uplifted.

2. My papers are all neatly filed/organised.

3. My home is clean and tidy.

4. I surround myself with beautiful things that inspire me.

5. I live in the geographical place I prefer.

6. I love my home.

7. I have a room or an area of my home that is my space to recharge.

———

8. My bed is made daily.

9. I have healthy plants or fresh flowers in my home.

10. My wardrobe and cupboards are well organised and uncluttered.

11. Everything in my home is something I want or need; if not, I give it to a charity shop or recycle it.

12. Everything works well in my home; if not, I fix it.

My Body:

1. I drink plenty of water every day.

2. My alcohol intake is within the recommended limits.

3. I only have one or two cups of coffee a day.

4. I have at least five servings daily of fruit and vegetables.

5. I only have one dessert or chocolate 'treat' a day.

6. I get some kind of exercise daily.

7. I take some time every day to relax and breathe deeply.

8. I am at a weight that feels good to me.

9. Every day I dress and present myself in a way that allows me to feel my best.

10. I get regular medical check-ups and ensure my blood pressure and cholesterol are within healthy ranges.

My Emotional and Mental Wellbeing:

1. I make sure my self-talk is positive, and give myself encouraging, helpful messages.

2. I am conscious of and grateful for all the blessings in my life.

3. I start every day with a positive, happy intention and focus.

4. I end each day with thoughts about everything that went well that day, what I'm proud of, what I'm grateful for.

5. I take excellent care of myself, identify a list of daily actions that will make me feel good and follow them.

6. I have something to look forward to every day.

7. I remember to enjoy the present moment.

8. I always have a good book on the go.

9. I have a plan of fun things I want to do in my free time.

10. I have a 'toolkit' of helpful actions/resources for challenging times.

My Money:

1. I have a spending plan for each month and follow it.

2. I have a reserve of at least three months' living expenses in an instant-access account.

3. I know how much I am financially worth.

4. I have a financial plan for the year.

5. I am now, or will soon be, on a track towards financial independence, however I define that.

6. I am on track with pension planning.

7. I do not worry about money.

8. I spend money in areas that are wise investments, however I define that.

9. I do not let financial fears prevent me from following my desired paths in life.

10. I am well insured.

11. I have an up-to-date will.

My Relationships:

1. I have no loose ends with relationships from the past.

2. I have forgiven those people who have hurt me.

3. I have a positive relationship with my parents and siblings.

4. I have a circle of friends with whom I enjoy spending time.

5. I have cultivated a professional network of people I respect.

6. I have a soulmate.

7. I value my relationships and put energy into maximising them, whatever that means.

8. I tell people how they can satisfy me.

9. I make quality time to spend with my family and friends as a priority.

10. I make love my highest priority.

My Work:

1. I love my work.

2. I have identified my vocation and am actively pursuing it.

3. I leverage my strengths at work.

4. I am an inspiring leader at work.

5. My work reflects who I am.

6. My work/life balance works well for me.

7. My work energises me.

---

8. I challenge myself at work to reflect my potential.

9. I continually learn and grow at work to maximise my performance.

10. I am happy with the financial rewards from my work.

These checklists are similar to those I encourage my coaching clients to work through, but feel free to amend the categories and the statements within them to ones that speak more to you, if any of those I've suggested don't resonate with you personally. The main thing to remember is that even if each point individually may seem insignificant, collectively, a number of unchecked points will drain your energy and make it hard, perhaps impossible, for you to achieve great things. Loose ends are really quite treacherous when it comes to moving forward and creating sustainable success.

The best way I've found to systematically work through these points and significantly build positive momentum is to turn it into a bit of a game. Adapt my checklist so it feels right for you and your life, then each week, choose the three easiest points to work through so that you can tick them off at the end of the week. As the weeks progress and your score rises, you will feel better, more energised and more positive, and you will be better able to tackle the more stubborn or difficult points at the end of the programme. Chart your scores on a graph so that you see the number rising each week, creating checkboxes for each item to tick as you achieve it.

Identifying and eliminating energy drains is guaranteed to make you feel good, confident and positive, and will give you that crucial positive momentum you need to turn challenges into opportunities, to go on your hero's journey towards your dream destination.

Now let's look at some other areas I recommend working through in order to create the feelgood factor and move forward happily towards your goals.

MANAGING FEAR

Fear is often an invisible accompanying presence in our lives, but it can be paralysing, inhibiting and, at the very least, draining. So when it comes to identifying what elements in your life and in your thinking might be preventing you from moving forward, understanding, reducing and, ideally, eliminating fear as far as possible is fundamentally important.

How does fear present itself? Well, we can be afraid of success, afraid of failure, afraid of repeating mistakes from the past. Conversely, we need courage to embark on ambitious goals and changes. We need to understand our fear, name it and try to transcend it as much as possible.

Fear of failure

Fear of failure can stop us from even attempting something new and exciting.

If you have a dream of something you really want, something that makes your heart lift, it can be a refuge to retreat to in life's more challenging moments – a fantasy to inspire you when you're feeling down. And the worry that if you try to turn your dream into reality, you might not succeed can feel very frightening indeed. Because if you try to bring the dream to life and fail, you will then lose even the fantasy of positive change. However, and this is a big however, the power of a dream to make you happy and change your life is intrinsically limited indeed. A dream deferred or put off indefinitely represents a waste of your life, a waste of your amazing potential. Yet with the right preparation, focus and support, you can succeed in turning your dream into reality – if it's the right dream for you in the first place. The key to success lies in approaching the process methodically, carefully, deliberately and constructively.

Fear of success

Fear of success can be paralysing too. You can want to achieve something and make spectacular changes, and yet also be fearful of change itself, of disrupting the status quo, perhaps even concerned about how others in your life might react to the new, improved you. Sometimes, your self-esteem might be damaged or at least dented and you may feel somehow unworthy of shining success. Sometimes, the familiar can be very reassuring, even if it's limiting and claustrophobic, and it takes real courage to determine to propel yourself forward out of your comfort zone into a new life of possibilities.

For example, one of my recent clients spent years feeling stifled in an oppressively uncommunicative and unloving marriage. There was no intellectual connection, no chemistry, little shared affection and fun. He knew he wanted more from a relationship and yet he was afraid of venturing out into a new world of being single after twenty years of marriage. Happily, with coaching support, he found the courage to take the steps he had so wanted to take for years. Working together, we clarified what his vision of a happy relationship looked like and established that he was so fundamentally incompatible with his current partner that the marriage was unlikely ever to come close to what he most wanted. We also came up with some strategies to help him deal with his fears and anxieties.

Life on the other side of this client's marriage is happier than he imagined it could be. Now dating someone whose company he is thoroughly enjoying, training to run a half-marathon and feeling re-inspired at work, he is delighted he found the courage to face his fears and stride forward.

Another client recently got a huge promotion, and even though it was in the industry he had most wanted to join, and was a role he had aspired to, when the reality of the opportunity presented itself, fear of failure or fear of success (or perhaps a mix of the two) temporarily blocked him, until we strategised on how he could move forward confidently to his new professional future. Now, of course, he's thriving and is exhilarated by every new challenge and opportunity. And he's delighted that he didn't stay in the safe but limiting confines of his previous role and industry.

With fear of success, the most important breakthrough is simply to realise that you have this fear and that it's having a negative effect on your progress. Once you identify it, you can come up with a plan to get around it and prevent it from derailing you. That might mean creating a new script to read to yourself each time you notice that you're feeling anxious. What realistic and reassuring messages can you convey to encourage yourself forward? You might want to look at your personality type (see p. 137) and see if there are any clues here or areas you can consciously work on to help yourself move forward. A precise and practical plan broken down into baby steps will give you the traction you need to overcome the potentially paralysing effect of fear of success.

———

Fear of repeating mistakes from the past

Another kind of fear can arise from your past. Perhaps you have limiting beliefs from the past that may not have been properly examined, unpacked and defused, and that are no longer true for your life in the present moment. Perhaps you've made mistakes (haven't we all?) and are afraid that you are somehow doomed to repeat them. As a consequence, you might be dodging metaphorical landmines, instead of confidently striding forward in healthy new directions.

For example, it might be that because your previous marriage failed, you are now afraid to commit to marrying again, even though you love your new partner, are very compatible with them and know that you have an entirely different relationship from the one you had with your ex-spouse.

The point here is to remember to refresh your thinking. *The Go-Between* by L. P. Hartley, opens with the very telling words: 'The past is a foreign country. They do things differently there.' Your present absolutely does not need to be defined by your past, and if you limit yourself in this way, you are in effect trying to move forward in your life while tracking heavy iron chains around your feet. To continue the foreign country theme, it's as if you're in China, for example, and you think that by speaking English more loudly, you will be able to make yourself understood.

The way forward here is to understand how the past has shaped you and to understand equally who and where you are now in your life. What's possible for you now depends on how open you are to shaping and creating your life henceforth. Usually, understanding this fear of repeating mistakes from the past is the first step to liberating yourself from any limitation, and preparing yourself to move forward to a happy, positive, successful, dynamic and, above all, fulfilling future.

Fear of commitment can simply reflect a framework of thinking based on a past you've outgrown, and it can prevent you from living a complete, whole-heartedly integrated life. I recently advised a client to 'make love, not excuses!' And there's no doubt that love and fear don't belong together; love means being brave and stepping forward on to a new journey of possibilities and adventure, whereas fear can sabotage you and limit your happiness and development. Once acknowledged and understood, it should be defused.

If you identify with this or similar scenarios, I invite you to rewrite your mental script and get rid of the emotional baggage that weighs you down and costs you so much in extra charges. As you know, on some journeys, the excess baggage charge can ruin your trip!

You need to find the courage to leave the familiar, get out of the harbour of limitation for the uncharted open sea of the possible and embark on your adventure. Leaving the shore involves exploring the art of the possible, not taking reckless risks, but creating a firm foundation for your journey.

GETTING YOUR NEEDS MET

We all have needs. It goes with the territory of being human. Yet if you ask someone what their key needs are – and we're not talking about basic physical needs here, like air and water, but emotional needs, which vary between individuals – the chances are that you will be met with a confused look, or an uncomprehending shrug.

I've noticed from the thousands of clients I've worked with over the years that people prefer not to acknowledge that they have needs, fearing that admitting this makes them seem 'needy' to themselves or to others, or that it makes them appear vulnerable and weak. If you don't recognise and meet your needs, however, they manipulate you insidiously from the sidelines. It's your unmet needs that cause you to overreact and turn a calm discussion into a heated one. It's your unmet needs that can (and will) sabotage you professionally and personally, that will undermine you every which way you turn. And apart from undermining you, they will also drain your energy, just like the loose ends

I was referring to earlier. In fact, unmet needs are really just emotional loose ends, but powerful and potentially destructive manipulators of our behaviour.

If you recognise your very natural needs, understand them and look after yourself by taking steps to get them met, you defuse their destructive power and tame them into neutral, innocent parts of your personality that simply need to be taken care of.

In my first few months working with new clients, we always start by identifying and eliminating energy drains, and establishing what their needs are and how to meet them (along with understanding their personality, but more of that later). Typically, I find that once people start taking steps to get their needs met, they quickly feel happier, more positive and much more energised.

Just as an aside, let me briefly explain the difference between needs and values, as they're often confused. Needs are non-negotiable for you; they are fundamental requirements in your life in order for you to feel OK. If your needs aren't being met, you are very limited in what you can strive for. Values, on the other hand, are qualities that inspire and excite you, themes that light you up and make you want to jump out of bed in the morning. In the next chapter, I will explain how to identify your values, which is a much more straightforward process once your needs are met.

———

Identifying your needs

So how do you identify your needs? Start by brainstorming all the words that occur to you as possible needs. Write down as many as possible, perhaps as many as fifty. Examples might be:

- Security
- Abundance
- To be loved
- To be desired
- To be cherished
- To excel
- To lead
- Family
- To have fun
- Adventure
- Stability
- To learn
- To be well regarded
- Excitement
- To be admired

- To be connected

- Structure

- To love

- To mentor

- To achieve

Once you've made as long a list as possible, choose the ten to twelve needs that most resonate with you. Once you've chosen, consider them more deeply and narrow them down to the three or four needs that feel absolutely fundamental to you.

Don't worry about getting the needs 'right'. There isn't a science to this process, and chances are that if you've shortlisted four needs, they are important enough for you to get huge benefit from taking care of them.

I can't overestimate how important it is to get your needs met before you start thinking about your values, and before you start trying to achieve stretching goals. If your needs aren't met, your energy is being drained and you're not running on all cylinders; that means you're not able to tap into all your power and potential. And you need to be able to be your best in order to do amazing things. So this is a crucial first step.

Psychologist Abraham Maslow, author of *Motivation and*

Personality, is well known for his theory about the hierarchy of needs. He envisages human development and self-improvement as a triangle or pyramid shape. Survival needs, i.e. physical needs like food, water and sleep, are at the bottom of the triangle. Clearly, if those needs aren't being addressed, you have to focus on them in order to stay alive, and you don't have the luxury of considering your emotional needs. Equally, then, if your emotional needs aren't being met, you won't be happy or effective, you won't be able to move up the pyramid towards self-fulfilment or self-actualisation. For our purposes, if your emotional needs aren't met, it will mean that you can't achieve your goals or turn challenge into opportunity.

Once you've identified your top four needs, I invite you to reflect on how and why they're important to you – how you feel when they are met, and what happens when they're not, and how you've seen those needs affect your experience in life at different stages.

Next, ask yourself these questions:

1. **What two small, measurable changes can I make to get each need met in the next two months?** You should come up with eight changes altogether, and make sure they are small enough to be achievable within two months. Then, get going on your eight changes, putting a mark in your calendar, coaching

journal or diary to indicate what needs to happen by when in order for each goal to be achieved. In other words, suppose one need is to feel good, and your goal to partially meet that need is to lose fourteen pounds in two months. In this example, consider what you need to do to achieve that and make a plan for yourself. So to lose two pounds a week, think about the eating and exercise regime you will start and how you will chart your course and progress.

2. **What are other people doing that is currently stopping me from getting a need met?** Can you gently let them know and ask them to stop, reminding them when they forget?

3. **What am I doing that is compromising my need?** Identify whatever this is and decide to stop it now!

4. **What can I ask other people to do for me to help me get my need met?** For example, if one of your needs is to be cherished, can you ask your partner to buy you flowers or a special small gift once a week or to tell you that he/she loves you every day in a heartfelt way? Try to ask them to do whatever it is you're requesting on a regular basis. If one of your needs, for example, is to be recognised, you could ask your boss to give you positive, constructive feedback on your performance once a month over an informal coffee.

---

5. **What can I do myself to meet each of my needs?**
You will find that with some focused attention, you can significantly improve your feelgood factor and energy levels. Just remember that if you understand your needs and take care of them as much as possible, they will cease to be a negative influence manipulating you from behind the scenes, and will become a neutral part of who you are.

SELF-CARE AND SELF-ESTEEM

Understanding your needs and taking care of them is part of a healthy self-care routine, as is eliminating energy drains and clearing up loose ends in your life.

Good self-esteem is something we often talk about, but the actual process of achieving and improving it is often rather vague and inchoate.

We need good self-esteem to feel confident about our abilities to create positive change in our lives, and equally we need healthy self-esteem to actually move forward on the journey towards achieving exciting goals. And the good news is that I've discovered through my coaching work that self-esteem is something you can systematically develop with the correct approach.

Let's look at the formula I mentioned earlier: self-care + self-respect = self-esteem. What this actually means in practice is that if you combine the actions of self-care by looking after yourself practically in some of the ways we've looked at already, with the mental thought process of thinking about yourself positively and with respect, the combined power of action and thought leads to high self-esteem. So by practising good self-care, you are giving yourself the message that you are someone worth taking care of. Conversely, by neglecting yourself, you are giving yourself the damaging message that you're not someone worth looking after. Even if you think of yourself with respect and in a positive framework, the impact of giving yourself a mixed message with your self-care is intrinsically undermining.

By putting yourself first, being healthily selfish and not sacrificing your own needs for those others, you will find that you will be more present, more sensitive, more helpful and more productive in all your relationships. It's paradoxical, but true. Think of the advice from flight attendants during the safety drills, for example: if you are travelling with infants or children, put on your own oxygen mask first so that you are better able to help them; if you run out of oxygen before you have your mask on, none of you will survive. This can be a helpful practical reminder of the importance of empowering yourself first in order to then be more helpful to others.

So what does your self-care plan look like? What are you currently doing and what can you do more of, on a daily, weekly, monthly and annual basis? I plan my self-care appointments and diarise them three months in advance. That means that I work out regularly with my trainer every week, actually get to my Friday yoga class, get my hair cut before it desperately needs it and, importantly, I'm not practically at the bottom of my own to-do list.

How much do you respect yourself at the moment? What messages are you giving yourself about you? Do any of those messages need rescripting in order to become more positively encouraging?

On a scale of one to ten, where one is the lowest score, where would you rate your self-esteem currently? What can you do in the areas of self-care and self-respect to raise it by two points in the next two months?

Create a toolkit of happy habits

One of the most powerful practices to embrace for energising self-care is to identify a list of daily habits you can follow to make you feel good. Putting yourself at the end of your to-do list means, in practice, that you will literally never get around to yourself. But making it a priority to cultivate your happy habits each day will help you to accomplish everything else on your list with more ease and grace.

———

I suggest to my clients that they identify ten things they would like to commit to doing each day that will improve their wellbeing. Everyone's list is different, and the key thing is that the habits you choose are good *for* you and also feel good *to* you. So destructive habits clearly have no place here.

What is on *your* list? Here are examples of some of the habits my clients have chosen in the past, just to get you going on your own list (and it's fine to choose fewer than ten to begin with, if you prefer):

- Go for a walk in nature each day, even if it's only for ten minutes.

- Catch up with one friend every day for a coffee or chat.

- Read your newspaper/magazine of choice from cover to cover.

- Practise yoga or a short meditation.

- Choose an intention for the day.

- At the end of the day, reflect on ten things you enjoyed.

- Take a bath or shower with your favourite aromatherapy products.

- Read a book.

- Play with your children.

- Have a glass of amazing wine.

- Make love (or at least kiss)!

- Do a challenging crossword.

- Read a bedtime story to your child.

- Take ten minutes to enjoy your preferred coffee.

- Wear something you love.

- Chart your top priorities for the day.

- Diffuse aromatherapy oil at home to make your room smell wonderful.

- Remember to breathe deeply.

- Have something to look forward to every day.

- Cook dinner with your partner and chat.

Get the picture? Take time to reflect on the daily habits that will bring a pleasurable sparkle to your day, and note them in the space below or in your journey notebook if you've chosen to use one:

My Daily Happy Habits Chart

- _____

- _____

- _____

_____

- _____
- _____
- _____
- _____
- _____
- _____
- _____

With continued practice, you will find that your happy habits become part of your normal routine, though this does take some time.

Choose a theme for each month

Another idea is to choose a theme for each month and adapt your monthly habits so that they support your theme. For example, April could be your month for getting physically fit, and your habits could be adapted accordingly to support that focus. May could be your month for friendship and your habits could reflect that. You could, in fact, choose a theme for each month of the year, select habits that support them, and at the end of the year select the ten habits that have contributed most to your wellbeing.

Create a toolkit for challenging times

Another useful idea is to create an emergency toolkit for challenging times. Whether the resources in your toolkit reflect what's true for you at the moment, or whether you keep them to one side for when you need them, it can be empowering and reassuring to know that you're prepared for the times when it's most difficult to venture out and identify supportive resources. For women, the toolkit could include a couple of inspiring books that always make you feel good, the contact details for a great spa therapist or beauty therapist, a favourite magazine (I think Oprah Winfrey's magazine *O* is wonderfully uplifting), delicious chocolate, a funny DVD, a CD of music you enjoy, even a letter to yourself with reminders of what to focus on when things feel hard. For men, it might be the rugby schedule of your local team, a computer game that distracts you, a map to a local nature walk you've always wanted to go on, a book by your favourite author, etc. The point is to create a list that resonates with you.

CREATING POSITIVE MOMENTUM

In order to do extraordinary things, you need to be ready to move forward with your life. Like the surfer I described in the

Introduction, you need to be ready to catch your wave. It's not the time to be dithering, doubting, procrastinating or feeling blocked. In fact, it's a real 'seize the moment' occasion.

And being ready to catch your wave means being in a physical, emotional, and mental place of readiness, where you feel good, energetic and liberated from past clutter, prepared to reclaim lost or missing parts of yourself and be the person you have the potential to be.

Positive momentum is all-important. The more unnecessary energy blocks you clear from your life in the form of loose ends, physical and mental clutter, unmet needs and unexamined fear, the more confident, and ready you will feel to embrace positive change. As you work through the exercises I have outlined in this chapter, you will feel a growing sense of lightness, excitement, confidence and positive possibility. Equally significant is the enhanced ability you will experience to enjoy each moment of your journey, to live in the present while knowing that you're headed in inspiring directions.

With my coaching clients, I spend the first three months of our work together on exactly this focus of building a happy foundation, along with analysing personality, and I know from experience that the brilliant results and changes people want to create for themselves need to be founded on this clear platform for success.

One of my current clients, Simon, works in finance and

is currently searching for a fulfilling new role. As I write this, we have worked together for two months, and he tells me that his energy levels have recently rocketed because of how we're approaching his preparation for change, and that his confidence and peace of mind are helping him to maximise meetings and interviews.

Whatever your individual situation and challenge, please feel reassured that you can get your journey off to a hugely positive start by building the foundation of happiness we have been exploring.

EMBRACING POSITIVE CHANGE

Once you have achieved a fabulous foundation for change, as outlined above, you need to believe. You need to be convinced that it really is possible for you to accomplish amazing things, to feel successful, happy, fulfilled and even blissful. You need *faith*.

I find that lots of people don't really believe that sustainable and dramatic positive change is possible for them. It's almost as if they choose to protect themselves from disappointment by refusing to believe wholeheartedly that they can be incredibly happy and fulfilled. Or they pretend that they believe, but on closer scrutiny it is clear that they don't, and that they are sabotaging their own efforts in various insidious, underhand ways.

What's important is that you choose goals that are a perfect fit for you, goals that reflect your personality and values and leverage your strengths. Rather than choosing theoretical, joyless goals, you need to articulate those to which your mind, heart and spirit sing an unequivocal 'yes'.

Ultimately, making each day and each step of your journey as joyful and as pleasurable as possible is a creative way of living your life as art, making space for synchronicity and flow. Your experience of walking along your path in the present, with intentionality, awareness and wonderful self-care is every bit as important as the satisfaction and pleasure you will feel arriving at each dream destination.

In the next chapter we will focus on you understanding yourself in clear, three-dimensional depth in order to define the path that is perfect for you.

CHECKLIST OF ACTION STEPS IN THIS CHAPTER

☐ Create your own feelgood factors. Explore, list, map, draw what makes you happy …

☐ Outline your life so far, drawing a map of the journey.

☐ Identify and systematically work on eliminating the areas

---

that need to be sorted out and that drain your energy in each aspect of your life. Compile a list that you can work through, choosing a few small items to focus on each week.

☐ Identify your top ten to twelve needs, then narrow this down to the key three or four.

☐ Ask yourself what changes you can make in the next two months to get your key needs met.

☐ Produce an extraordinary self-care plan.

☐ Create your toolkit of daily happy habits (and follow your list!)

☐ Prepare your emergency toolkit for challenging times.

CHAPTER 4

Who Are You, Really?

What if you could find your own personalised treasure map, full of clues to uncover and discover your heart's desire, your top three wishes, your pot of gold at the end of your metaphorical rainbow? Well, you can, and I'm about to show you how.

There are several exercises in this chapter, so I suggest you have a notebook handy to work with as you read, and that you stop, reflect, and write whenever you feel inspired to do so. In fact, if you haven't already done so, this is a good point at which to buy a dedicated coaching journal – one you find appealing, maybe with different sections.

In order to have balance, harmony, and happiness in your life, and to be as successful as you have the potential to be, you need to understand your personality type so that you

---

know who you are and what you have to work with. You also have to analyse your strengths, rather than take them for granted, and create a plan to leverage them to their full advantage. As we saw in the previous chapter, you need to know what your key needs are and endeavour to meet them, so that they don't sabotage you from behind the scenes, causing you to act out because of unconscious and unfulfilled drivers. And you need to clarify your values, discover what excites you and lights you up with joy, and then orientate your life so that it revolves around these qualities and values.

Understanding who you are at your best will also allow you to discover your ideal focus or purpose in life, to sort out what matters and what doesn't and to recognise what you should focus your time, energy, and attention on, and what you should ignore or forget about.

Whether you are facing external change, like a relationship breakdown or redundancy at work, an internal call to adventure urging you forward to explore new directions, or simply want to make positive and life-defining changes in your life, knowing who you are and what is in your treasure box is fundamental. It is the magic key that will help you to unlock your success and happiness. Shining a light on who you are at your best and deliberately cultivating that unique individual will, in turn, allow you to shine and be brilliant. And the benefits of this clarity will enhance both your personal and professional life, accelerating your success in both areas, allowing them to be mutually enhancing rather than competing. Your clarity about who you are and what is right for you will be your candle or torch as you go on your journey through Dante's dark wood of change towards your dream destination on the other side.

YOUR PERSONALITY TYPE

If you were sitting with a friend right now, enjoying a coffee or drink and having a chat, and they were to ask you to describe your personality, how would you respond? Would you immediately be able to convey what makes you you in a few clear sentences? Or would you pause and wonder what to say next? I tried this experiment myself with a friend yesterday. His response was, 'Well, when I'm in such-and-such a situation, I respond like this . . .' I countered with, 'But how would you describe your personality? Is your first response thinking, feeling or intuiting?' Again, he paused and wasn't sure how to answer my question. And most of us hesitate similarly when we try to convey our essential self clearly and succinctly.

We think we know ourselves, but do we really? Are we not perhaps too close to ourselves to have a clear perspective? Personality profiling is one of the first things I do with new coaching clients. Invariably, I find that people are excited and struck by how many confusing things fall into place when they truly understand themselves. Patterns that seem unaccountable, situations that stress them out, relationship conflicts, all suddenly make sense and come into focus when seen through the lens of a clearly understood personality type framework.

Most people don't know themselves very well at all. And not knowing really limits your ability to excel, to be brilliant, to find your unique happiness blueprint. Yet understanding yourself – particularly when you're facing changes, transitions and challenges or trying to create something new and wonderful in your life – is fundamental in showing you the best path forward and how to walk on it.

So how do you discover your personality? And how can you use the insights to create magic in your life? I suggest you take out your coaching journal at this point and take an hour to explore your personality. What are all the adjectives that you could use to describe yourself? How have other people described you? What makes you happy? What makes you sad? What inspires you? What upsets or irritates you? What qualities do you value in others? It can be useful to write uninterrupted in a free-flowing way for twenty to thirty minutes, writing everything that comes into your mind without censoring yourself. You may be surprised by some of the insights you come up with.

PERSONALITY TESTS

Some of the better-known personality assessments are the Lüscher Colour Personality, the Big Five personality test, Firo B (Fundamental Interpersonal Relations Orientation Behaviour), and MBTI or Myers-Briggs.

In the Lüscher Colour Personality system, each person is associated with particular colours and qualities. The Big Five personality test assesses people on five key dimensions – extraversion vs introversion, confidence vs sensitivity, detail-conscious vs unstructured, tough-minded vs agreeable and conforming vs creative – and everyone is somewhere on a scale between the extremes in each polarity. Firo b looks at the extent to which people express three basic needs – inclusion, control and affection – and how much they desire to have others express those qualities to them. MBTI or Myers-Briggs is based on Carl Jung's personality typing and uses four main polarities: extraversion/introversion (the focus of our orientation, inner or outer), thinking/feeling, sensing/intuiting (how we gather information) and judging/perceptive (how we react to the world and how we make decisions).

Many of you will already have taken some kind of personality test, perhaps at work or for professional assessment of some kind. One of the problems with many personality-typing systems (see box) is that they can be quite reductive and even simplistic, and may not give you much new information about what makes you you. For example, many of you would already know if you are introverted or extroverted, and a personality test stating this is not going to be particularly illuminating. The other problem is that people can sometimes take personality typing as an excuse not to try to improve or grow – as in, 'I'm a red type and so I'm prone to passionate outbursts and losing my temper, and can't help it. It's just who I am.'

The personality profiling system I use myself with clients is brilliant because it challenges you to be your absolutely best self, and shows you the individualised path to get there. It also manages to be simultaneously complex and simple, multi-dimensional and yet, when you understand its framework, straightforward. It's called the Enneagram and I thoroughly recommend it to you as, in my opinion, the most practical, profound and dynamic approach available. Of course, if you already use another personality-profiling system and are happy with that, by all means stay with it, but just make sure that you are using the insights as part of your dynamic plan to get you where you want to go.

The Enneagram

The Enneagram is an extraordinarily useful way to develop greater self-understanding and personal growth. Rather than put you in a box, like so many other personality systems, it actually shows you the box you're already in, and how to get out of it. It allows you to be conscious of how and why you behave as you do, and how to consciously improve. It also shows you what can push you into unhelpful behaviour or trigger unhelpful reactions.

The modern Enneagram (from the Greek *ennea*, meaning nine, and *gammos*, meaning something written or drawn) was first conceived of by spiritual teacher and psychologist Oscar Ichazo and elaborated by psychologist Claudio Naranjo, based on earlier teachings of the mystic and teacher G. I. Gurdjieff. Naranjo brought the Enneagram to the USA, where it was further developed by Don Riso, among others. It outlines nine personality types, each of which corresponds to one of nine points on the Enneagram, a geometric figure (below).

Enneagram with Riso-Hudson Type Names

The nine types have different names, depending on the interpreter of the Enneagram: Type 1 is known as the Reformer, Perfectionist or Idealist; Type 2 as the Helper or Carer; Type 3 as the Achiever or Producer; Type 4 as the Individualist or Romantic; Type 5 as the Investigator or Observer; Type 6 as the Loyalist or Troubleshooter; Type 7 as the Enthusiast or Adventurer; Type 8 as the Challenger or Top-dog; and Type 9 as the Peacemaker.

Various authors have written about the Enneagram, coming up with different interpretations and approaches. I studied with Don Riso and Russ Hudson of The Enneagram Institute in the USA, and find their approach to the Enneagram as a personal and professional development framework hugely inspiring. One of their insights into the dynamic nature of the Enneagram is identifying and exploring the Levels of Development within each type, depending on how emotionally and mentally healthy the individual is. In other words, two Type Ones can vary completely, depending on where they are in what Riso and Hudson view as the nine-point scale (where nine is extremely unhealthy and one is extremely healthy and balanced). For example, a very balanced Type 1 will be positively idealistic, intent on making the world a better place and probably working and inspiring others to do so – like Mahatma Ghandi. In a very unhealthy Type 1, the idealism manifests in being critical, judgmental, punitively harsh to themselves and to others.

Working with the Enneagram for personal development
If you're interested in working with the Enneagram for personal development and to support yourself through change, the first step is to decide which of the nine types you are (see below). To find out which type you are, I suggest you take the RHETI Enneagram Test on The Enneagram Institute website (see Resources, p. 231). The test takes approximately forty minutes and can be taken online. If your Enneagram profiling scores are slightly ambiguous, it might be helpful to read through the more detailed descriptions of each type in an Enneagram book (see Reommended Reading, p. 232) to determine which type you are. Although each of us has a bit of all nine types within us, ultimately we are all predominantly one type, and understanding what that is will give you valuable insight for working successfully through change.

Once you feel you've got your type right, decide where you are currently on the level of development for that type, and make notes on how you can work towards becoming the most healthy version of it: what to do more of, what to do less of, what to start doing, what to stop doing, signs of stress to watch out for and what action plan you can put in place for yourself to support yourself through challenging times and times of transition in your life and to take advantage of opportunities.

The nine Enneagram types

Let's take a look at each of the nine Enneagram types in detail to identify what they are and how you can support yourself to embrace change and maximise opportunities by understanding your type.

Type 1: the Reformer, Perfectionist or Idealist

Type 1s are extremely idealistic, often to the point of being perfectionist. They set very high standards, both for themselves and for others, so that their friends, colleagues and partners can sometimes feel that they fall short of what's expected of them. Some Type 1s want to change the world (Mahatma Ghandi was, apparently, a Type 1) and often have reforming zeal. Others just want to maximise themselves, their career, their workplace. Idealism is also fundamental to Type 1s and they tend not to believe in compromise or doing things by halves.

The key lesson for Type 1s is to be more gentle on themselves, less perfectionist and self-critical and also less judgmental towards others. Make sure that your idealistic aspirations are reflected in positive action, that you engage at your workplace in ways that give you a chance to use and express your interest in improving things, systems, structures and people for the better. And that your personal life is commensurate with your high standards, but not a victim of them. For example, Type 1 mothers may tend to overload their children with music practice and other after-school activities in their desire to help them excel. It's sometimes good to lighten up, to make time to play with your children – just fifteen to twenty minutes on the floor with them playing tiddlywinks, or joining in on a Wii-fit balance game.

When going through change, challenges and maximising new opportunities, the key point for a Type 1 is to lighten up and not be obsessive – to go for good enough, rather than perfect, so that you actually get things done. Remember to create balance in your life, to look after and not sideline yourself and your needs in your attempt to move mountains and achieve great things practically perfectly (or perfectly perfectly in your case). It's also very important that Type 1s are less self-critical when trying to navigate change. Instead of focusing on all the things you could be doing to move forward that you are failing to do, concentrate on the things that you *are* doing to help yourself, and remember to encourage yourself and be gentle with your self-talk.

Type 2: the Helper or Carer
If you are a Type 2, the Carer, you are inclined to focus on looking after other people rather than taking care of yourself, and this tendency can lead to energy drain, even

burnout, at which point Type 2s can resort to manipulation, emotional blackmail and even to aggressive, angry outbursts. So it's important to consciously prioritise your own wants and needs, to deliberately look after yourself physically, emotionally and spiritually.

In times of change and transition, it is more important than ever for Type 2s to practise extraordinarily good self-care, and to really consider what you can do on a daily basis to look after yourself and give yourself energy back to use for your own development and life.

Type 3: the Achiever or Producer

Type 3s are so focused on achieving, excelling and getting ahead, that sometimes they put their feelings in a box on a high shelf, intending to get to them later when they aren't so busy achieving. However, they often don't get back to them. Even though Type 3 is very much a feeling type, being very heart-centred intrinsically, they can bracket their feelings to such an extent that they become alienated and estranged from them, unable to access the wisdom that their heart and their feelings can provide them.

So the key point for you if you are a Type 3 is to check in with your feelings, ask yourself what you are feeling, what your heart is saying, what feels true and right for you. Under pressure, Type 3s can tend to focus on how other people are perceiving and judging them, and can try, almost chameleon-like to be what they think the other person wants or expects them to be. The trick is, again, to get back in touch with your own truth, your own feelings. Otherwise, when under pressure, you risk turning into an achieving machine, burned out, inauthentic and personally drained.

Type 4: the Individualist or Romantic

Type 4s are intense, sensitive, intuitive, aesthetic and very feeling. They are often poets, writers, artists – expressively creative in different ways.

When under pressure or facing challenge, as a Type 4 you run the risk of drowning in your feelings, becoming very sad or very emotionally high. The key for 4s is to balance your feelings out with your thoughts and physical energy, so exercising regularly, making sure your thoughts are positive, creating habits and patterns that will support you through emotional turbulence are all important.

A practical and disciplined structure of daily and weekly activity will comfort and uplift 4s, giving you traction to emerge from feeling sad and stride forward towards making your dreams a reality. Here are some questions to ask yourself if you're a 4:

- What weekly, daily routine will support me through transition?

- How can I look after myself and get emotional support during challenging times of change?

It's important for Type 4s to be quite self-protective because of their sensitivity and to practise excellent self care. Coming up with a list of ten things you can do each day that will be good for you and that you'll enjoy (see p. 125) is a particularly useful exercise for sensitive 4s.

Type 5: the Investigator or Observer

Type 5s are the thoughtful, detached intellectuals, often so immersed in the mental challenges and subjects that engage them, that they can be a bit switched off from the demands of the practical, physical world and the people they are in a relationship with.

As a Type 5, who lives very much in their head, you'd benefit – especially when dealing with change and challenge – from connecting up with your emotions and with your physicality. Training for a half-marathon, joining a reading group or learning how to make home-made pizza, for example, would all be helpful practices to help you develop and maximise your positive opportunities for moving forward and achieving. It's important for you to get out of your head and into the practical world.

Type 6: the Loyalist or Troubleshooter

Type 6s are engaging, funny, loyal and conscientious people

who like to feel secure and in a structured framework professionally and personally where they know where they stand.

If you're a Type 6, you'll be prone to anxiety and self-doubt, and to living too much in your head (like types 5 and 7). You need to give yourself lots of positive reassurance when facing change. In order to grow and take best advantage of opportunities, you need to listen to your inner script – the messages you are giving yourself – and learn to rewrite it so that it becomes positive, encouraging and affirming.

You'd also do well to develop your self-trust, self-belief and self-esteem (see p. 55-93), learning to become internally resilient and confident, despite what's happening around you. Rather than automatically focusing on what might go wrong, you would benefit from looking at what is going right, and what you might do to encourage it to go even better. Cultivating trust and confidence are helpful practices for you too, clarifying your expectations and assumptions in your relationships.

Meditation or yoga or taking up daily walking in an effort to quiet and balance the mind are useful habits to support Type 6s through change.

Type 7: the Enthusiast or Troubleshooter
Type 7s are creative, enthusiastic, spontaneous and analytical. At their best they are fun-loving, engaging, lively and

entertaining. But under pressure, they tend to get scattered and superficial, distracted and pain-avoidant, disconnected from their feelings, caught up in a whirlwind of analysis which goes round and round their heads and leads them nowhere.

If you are a Type 7, you need to cultivate focus, discipline and depth, to put energy into staying with your feelings, rather than distracting yourself with superficial pleasures and to work through to positive solutions, rather than fantasising about the grass being greener somewhere else.

To make positive changes in your life, try to stay connected with your feelings and focus on the possibilities for depth and understanding in your life today. Resist the tendency to use your head to analyse endlessly. Being in nature, walking and exercise in general are all good activities to help ground and centre you, aligning your head with your heart and your physical self to bring you into balance and ready to move forward in your life.

A Type 7 client of mine used to paralyse himself into fear and inaction by going too much into his head and considering everything that might go wrong, then distracting himself from his anxiety by playing computer games and watching sports. Instead, he learned that to make exciting breakthroughs in his life he needed to connect with his heart and his feelings, walk by the river or in the park, do serious gardening in order to connect up his head, heart, and instincts and give himself the courage and forward momentum to make choices and move forward.

Type 8: the Challenger or Top-dog

Type 8s are often found in leadership positions, being naturally authoritative and powerful.

One of the gut-instinct types, as an 8 you'll be grounded and in touch with your instinctual knowing, and at your best can be a natural leader, charismatic, strong and commanding trust. When doing well, you can also be quite connected with your feelings, and have an innate loyalty and protectiveness that makes you great at looking after your family, your team and taking charge. You tend, however, to be unaware of just how much your innate strength can overpower and even overwhelm people, and need to be conscious of the degree of energy you project to others, learning to moderate your responses and use only as much energy and force as necessary. As a leader, you can sometimes terrify your direct reports who have different personality types, coming across as bullying and scary because of your force and intensity. And two Type 8 colleagues can inadvertently get into a mutually confrontational situation unless both are aware of the personality dynamics at play.

When under stress and facing change, you can neglect yourself, pushing yourself even harder than you push

WHO DO YOU WANT TO BE?

others. You'd benefit from reconnecting with your heart and with your tenderness, taking more care to nurture yourself, as well as others.

Type 9: the Peacemaker

Type 9s are usually gentle, peaceable and friendly; they are natural moderators and mediators, avoiding conflict at almost any cost. At their best, 9s have a lovely, inviting, peaceful energy and a natural ability to work with people to bring them together. When under stress, 9s tend to withdraw, close down and become passive, so desperate to avoid conflict that they move into avoidance altogether and emotionally and mentally withdraw, even shut down.

If you are a Type 9 and want to make positive things happen in your life, make sure that you are taking positive action, rather than waiting passively for something to happen to you. For example, one of my Type 9 clients is hoping to meet her life partner, but rather than being proactive about it, trying speed or online dating and attending social events, she says that the right person will show up when it's the right time. And while I do believe that 'Fate steps in and sees you through', as the song in *Pinocchio* goes, in order for life or synchronicity to meet you halfway, you need to take some action to get yourself in the right place to meet Fate on time. So you 9s would do well to consider what you can positively, proactively do –

how you can engage with life to move yourselves forward.

Each of us uses our hearts, our heads and our gut instinct to understand the world and to react to our lives, circumstances and relationships.

The Enneagram explains that three of the types outlined above (2, 3 and 4) are primarily heart-centred and will initially have a feeling reaction to and understanding of what is happening in their lives; they also need to consciously connect to their thought processes and to their instincts in order to create a balanced picture for themselves.

Types 5, 6 and 7 are primarily head-based, and can experience seemingly endless circulating mental analysis; they need to consciously connect up with their emotions and their gut instincts in order to balance themselves out and optimise their possibilities.

Types 8, 9 and 1 are the gut-instinct types, often having a visceral and intuitive knowing about what's happening to and around them; they need to bring in their feelings and their thoughts in order to be their best.

Each of the nine types is different in its individual personality road map. Understanding what type you are and how you react to the world, understanding your particular road map, equips you not only to learn how to cultivate your best self and take advantage of the natural strengths of your personality, but also to become more resilient in the face of stress and change. If you can be alert to the signs of stress within your personality type, while consciously trying to maximise and leverage your natural strengths, you can regroup and get back on track with minimal disruption, even in the face of a difficult external situation, like a relationship break-up or job loss.

Understanding the Enneagram type of significant people in your personal and professional life, as well as your own, is extraordinarily helpful for maximising your relationships. If you can, encourage them to work out what their type is, as outlined above; if that isn't possible, you might be able to make an educated guess, but be careful, because you may well get it wrong and your communication approach may then backfire and become counterproductive!

When I'm coaching professional teams, I always profile each person using the Enneagram, as it's usually transformative in terms of unlocking mutual understanding, appreciation and the ability to work together dynamically as part of the team.

How does the Enneagram help with career challenges?
Perhaps you are reading this book because your career feels stuck and you want to move ahead and get promoted, but feel blocked. You might feel you're in the right kind of work, possibly even in the right company or environment,

but that your career is still not advancing in the way or at the speed you would ideally like.

Knowing your Enneagram type allows you to manage your own career development by giving you insight into how you can shine at work and create harmony by putting yourself into a context that plays to your strengths and by helping you understand and manage your professional relationships.

Understanding the Enneagram framework and the personality type of your colleagues, managers and direct reports can also prove revelatory. After all, realising that everyone really speaks different languages helps you to understand why, say, certain colleagues are behaving as they are; it helps you to speak their language and to translate your own, so that they can connect more easily to you. It creates a common language through which to identify issues and find solutions, and is especially valuable for team and leadership development, conflict resolution and negotiation.

Working recently with the senior management team of one of my corporate clients, I saw first-hand how transformative it is for people to understand their own Enneagram type and that of their colleagues. For example, when a Type 2 and a Type 8 are working together, the 2 can find that the 8 is so forceful and direct that they feel overwhelmed, steamrollered, misunderstood and unappreciated. But if the 2 can communicate to their 8 colleague how important their feelings are to them, how sensitive to praise and criticism they are, the 8 can modify their tone and approach in order to get the best out of the working relationship. The 2 can practise being more direct and blunt with the 8, relying less on the language of feelings and more on action, in order to come across as more credible and authoritative.

With Enneagram insight, you are able to focus consciously on bringing out your best and working to your highest potential, understanding how to leverage the positives in your personality to create great connections and results, and also how to manage and avoid the pitfalls that can cause friction and misunderstanding.

An understanding of the Enneagram type of your colleagues allows you to maximise your relationship, showing you how to get the best out of them, how to build connections and, equally, not to take personally or get frustrated by behaviour you might find difficult.

In terms of dynamics, it's exciting to realise how understanding the spectrum of Enneagram types within a team can take it forward to new levels of co-operation and success, where you're actively and consciously working together to harness your individual and collective strengths to achieve greatness.

How does the Enneagram help with career change?
Are you in the right company, or even in the right profession? Perhaps you are reading this book because you want

to find a vocation you can feel passionate about, and are feeling increasingly convinced that you're not who or where you should be, workwise.

Just like individuals, professions and companies tend to have their own Enneagram type, and understanding what that is and how it relates to your personality type gives you tremendous insight into how to get the best out of your work context. It can also reveal whether you're actually in the wrong profession or perhaps in the wrong company, and that you could be much happier in another environment that fits more harmoniously with who you are.

If you study your Enneagram type in depth, it will help you to work out the environment and types of work that will bring out the best in you and play to your natural strengths, as well as those that may not be suited to you and which may prove to be a thankless struggle. It is helpful to look at the fit between your Enneagram type and the actual career you are considering or have chosen. For example, if you're a Type 2, you might naturally be suited to a helping profession, such as nursing or teaching. If you're a Type 1, you might do well working for a charity or non-profit organisation, although you can adapt your personality to many types of environment. Michael Goldberg's book, *The 9 Ways of Working*, provides more detail on using Enneagram insight to maximise your career. (See Resources and Recommended Reading, pp. 235-6)

After a talk I gave recently on the Enneagram at the Vitality Show in London, a lady came up to me and told me she had just had a powerful insight. She'd realised that she was in the wrong job for her personality type, and that she finally understood why her work felt so stressful, despite the fact that she enjoyed what she was doing. Working as a freelance journalist, she very much enjoyed researching and writing, but found the inherent uncertainty and unpredictability of the writing assignments quite draining and troublesome. She also missed working in an environment with a team of colleagues, and found working freelance a bit lonely. Aware now that she was an Enneagram Type 6 – the Loyalist – she could see that she would be much happier in a more structured and predictable environment, and that the insecurity of a freelance writing career was playing on her natural tendencies to worry and be anxious about what would happen next. The financial aspect was also proving challenging, and she realised that as an Enneagram Type 6 she would be much happier with a dependable salary. So even though she loved writing and enjoyed the intellectual challenge and scope of freelance assignments, the nature of the role was not a good fit for her personality needs.

Equally, understanding how your personality type fits with that of your company can be revelatory. For example, Type 4 is known as the Romantic or Individualist, and

Type 4 companies are known for their commitment to uniqueness, high quality, elegance and aesthetics. You could consider Chanel or the Ritz-Carlton hotels as the epitome of Type 4 companies. If you are also a Type 4, you will be naturally drawn to this type of environment and will be attuned to the values, aspirations and atmosphere it reflects. You should, therefore, find it easy to align your way of working, your sensibility and sense of what's important to the values and priorities of your company. On the other hand, if you have a personality type which is less in tune with your Type 4 employer, being aware of how your traits and orientations fit with those of your company will help to prevent many misunderstandings and tensions.

Similarly, you could look at the Civil Service as a Type 9 company, focused on harmony, co-operation and peace-keeping. So for a Type 8 – the Challenger – there may be real tension between their desire to make things happen and to lead the way, and the calmer, more bureaucratic atmosphere of their workplace.

Working with the Enneagram to improve your relationships
Type 8s are from Mars, Type 4s are from Venus. Or at least they might as well be, considering the potential for misunderstanding between different Enneagram types.

In order to build happier, more connected relationships, it helps dramatically to understand what type your colleague, friend, or partner is. But the first point to understand is that we aren't wrong because we're different. Whether they are operating primarily from a thinking orientation (Types 6, 7, 8), a feeling approach (2, 3, 4), or a gut-instinct 'knowing' (8, 9 and 1), it is crucial to understand their world and perspective. If, for example, you are a thinking type, and your partner is a feeling type, know that they are reacting to news and developments from that orientation, and that you need to speak their language in order to have the most positive and productive connection.

You need to travel to meet the other person in their world, understand where you and they are in terms of personality, and then build bridges between your world and theirs, helping you to understand, relate, and learn.

Conscious loving in your personal relationships

Clients often ask me which types are most compatible in personal relationships. The happy news, though, is that any Enneagram type is compatible with any other, depending on how emotionally/mentally healthy they are.

Within each Enneagram type, as I mentioned earlier, there is a dynamic spectrum of development. Any individual who is at the very healthy level of development within their type, can get along beautifully with healthy levels of any other type. It is when we start to go down the scale of awareness and development that we start to clash with other types, and some more than others at that point.

So being conscious of your own Enneagram type and how it affects your behaviour in personal relationships, gives you the map to bring out the best in both yourself and your partner.

If you are both aware of these dynamics and are present in the moment, you can practise conscious loving in your personal relationships and become closer and more in love every day.

If you can see where your partner or friend is coming from in terms of their personality and expectations, then together you can create effective communication and avoid the potential pitfalls and triggers that will lead you down the path of argument, misunderstanding and confrontation. The idea is to transcend the ego limitations of your personality, understand the other person and cultivate your heart connection.

There are 45 different relationship combinations of Enneagram types, each with its own unique configuration, i.e. 4s and 1s, 7s and 4s, etc. Understanding the characteristics of a particular combination provides almost instant illumination, and the ability to develop your closeness and communication ease over time. Each particular relationship combination provides its own brand of possibility and challenge. If you are interested in learning more, there is a discussion of the different variables which affect compatibility as well as an online type combinations matrix on the Enneagram Institute website (see Resources amd Recommended Reading, p. 235). In *Are You My Type, Am I Yours?*, Renee Baron and Elizabeth Wagele also explore the implications of different Enneagram relationship combinations and offer advice on how to maximise harmony and happiness. Interestingly, there is apparently a pattern in terms of the types that are most attracted to each other. For example, Baron and Wagele state that male 7s are most likely to choose a 2 or 4 for their romantic partner, whereas female 7s will go for a 9, followed closely by a 6, 7 or 8.

UNDERSTANDING YOUR NEEDS

Apart from knowing and working consciously with your personality type to support you moving forward and help you make change positive, it's also important to understand your needs, strengths and values.

Working Out What Your Needs Are

I can hear you asking, OK, but how do I know what my needs are? In Chapter 3 I asked you to make a list of your key needs in order to promote self-care and self-esteem and I suggest you take 30-45 minutes right now to do something similar here. Pick up your coaching journal/notebook, and, reflecting on your life so far, ask yourself: What are the qualities, experiences, things that feel completely and basically fundamental and non-negotiable, that if you don't have them, you won't feel happy? Try to write down as many words as you can initially. Here are some examples:

- Control
- Free
- Recognition
- Love
- Honesty
- Abundance
- Respect
- Being busy
- Safety
- Security
- Feeling cherished
- Order
- Perfection
- Loyalty

- Generosity
- Accomplishment
- Comfort
- Pleasure
- Fun
- Connection

This list could be much longer, as the list of needs you might have is virtually endless. The key thing is that you brainstorm as many words representing your needs as possible, and then considering very carefully, choose the top 3-5 that most resonate with you as significant and non-negotiable.

When you've got your list of your top few needs, I suggest you take another thirty minutes or so to write and explore in your notebook why those needs are important to you, what it feels like when you do and don't get them met and what you could do to stop your energy being drained by these factors. Also make a list of what changes you could make in the next three months, specific, measurable, achievable, small changes, to get each need met, coming up with at least two changes per need, and no more than four.

For example, if one of your needs is prosperity or abundance, ask yourself how prosperous/abundant you feel right now, what's it's been like in the past when you have or haven't felt this way, what or who (including yourself) is preventing or limiting you feeling that way at the moment ... And what changes can you make in the next few months to feel more prosperous? Examples of possible changes might be to negotiate a pay raise, to see a financial advisor and make a plan to get out of debt or increase your investments, to make and stick to a monthly spending plan, to sign up for a money-saving tips newsletter.

Whether you're trying to adjust and grow through unsettling change, or whether you're venturing forward in new and exciting directions (or both!), making sure that you get your needs met will give you a solid, sustaining and sustainable foundation for happy development in the direction of your dreams.

UNDERSTANDING YOUR STRENGTHS

Apart from establishing your personality type and learning how to work with it, and clarifying your needs and getting them met, identifying and leveraging your strengths is another crucial part of your change treasure map.

We all have particular strengths and talents – ways in which we naturally excel and are brilliant. Sadly, most of the time we don't really know what those strengths are, so we can't make the most of them to create exciting results.

Or, if we know what they are, we may take them for granted, and assume that because we are naturally gifted in particular ways, that everyone else is too, or that because our strengths come naturally to us, they are nothing special. Equally, we will notice strengths in other people and judge ourselves critically for not possessing the same qualities.

This is all wrong and very self-limiting. If you know what your strengths are, and ensure that you use them fully to achieve your goals, you give yourself a huge advantage and boost in moving forward. And again, especially in times of change and growth, you really need to draw on your strengths to live your potential.

So how do you identify your strengths? You might want to start by asking yourself what your biggest successes and achievements in your life so far have been, and what strengths you called on to create those results? This would be a good moment to take some time away from reading and go to your coaching journal for thirty to forty minutes or so in order to write down your thoughts, insights and reflections on your particular strengths.

After you've got a shortlist, you might want to ask people who know you best – your family, friends and colleagues – for their perceptions about your strengths. Add those to your list.

It's probably best if you reduce your list to about five strengths – enough to really flex and stretch, but not so many that it's overwhelming. If you're still not absolutely sure that you've identified your particular strengths, you might want to Google 'strengths' on the Internet, and find a strengths profiling test that you can do in order to get a report outlining your key talents. With my coaching clients, I use the book *Now, Discover Your Strengths* by Marcus Buckingham and Donald O. Clifton (See Resources and Recommended Reading pp. 235-6), which comes with a code for an online StrengthsFinder test. You may want to investigate this resource if you're not completely confident with the strengths list you outline in your coaching journal.

Assuming that you've now got your shortlist of strengths, and that you're happy they are pretty accurate, the next step is to ask yourself to what extent you are currently using the strengths you've identified in your personal and work life. You might want to use a percentage scale, for example; look at the results, and see where there is scope for leveraging each strength more fully in order to create outstanding results for yourself.

Let's say that one of your strengths is being strategic. The difference between using that strength to 40 per cent of its potential in your work versus 90 per cent is absolutely huge in its implications for your success. You might also be surprised to find that you are leveraging your strengths fairly well in your work life, but neglecting them in your personal life, or vice versa.

In any case, leveraging your strengths consciously, deliberately and fully is absolutely key to navigating change and creating breakthroughs in your life. It's definitely one of the prized jewels in your treasure chest, along with understanding your personality and your needs.

For example, supposing the positive change you are trying to create for yourself involves starting a new business. If one of your strengths is communication, then be sure to think about how you can actively engage your communication skills to get your business off to a great start – maybe by giving some talks, writing articles or holding a networking launch party. The point is that if you start with your strengths, of course also considering your personality, you will be much more likely to get fabulous results than if you make an action plan which doesn't maximise them. Why not take advantage of all the brilliance you have at your disposal? After all, it's by using our strengths that we can be most amazing, rather than managing our weaknesses and staying mediocre.

UNDERSTANDING YOUR VALUES

Values are the other secret ingredient in your treasure chest of possibilities. While your needs are more fundamental, not optional but essential, and getting them met stops your energy from draining out, reflecting your values in your life and work actually inspires you, filling you with energy and happiness, making you want to jump out of bed every day singing, 'Oh what a beautiful morning'.

As I mentioned earlier in the chapter, most people don't know what their values are, and mistakenly equate them with moral principles. So how do you identify your values?

Take out your coaching journal again, and give yourself about an hour to sit down quietly, ideally somewhere beautiful and inspiring – perhaps a garden or by the fire, depending on the season. Ask yourself what the happiest moments in your life have been so far. What led up to them? Where were you? What was happening? What qualities are represented by those experiences?

Make as long a list as possible of all the words that come to mind when you think about values. Typically, values are with us from when we're children, and so peak memories and experiences you absolutely loved as a child will give you important clues as to what your values might be. (For our purposes, these need not have any moral significance.) Examples are: loyalty, wholeheartedness, grace, radiance, adventure, family, learning, excellence, connection, love, doing the right thing, to improve, to build, to restore, sensuality, hedonism, fun, balance, beauty, spirituality ... the list is virtually endless.

Once you've identified about ten values that really feel

special to you, see if you can pick out the four that stand out as especially important. Sometimes, it helps to write about each one in your coaching journal, then to look back at what you've written to see which descriptions convey the most energy and enthusiasm. It can also be useful to reflect when each value has shown up in your life, and what immediate, instinctive associations you have with it.

Once you've chosen your four most important, write them in your coaching journal and also on a card that you will put somewhere prominent and visible, like on your desk at home, in your diary or even on your fridge door. The key is that you memorise your values and internalise them so that you always have them ready to act as a guide or signpost whenever you have choices to make.

Your values are of the utmost importance to your success in navigating change and turning challenge into opportunity. If you could ask each value what it would have you do, it would point you in the direction of your dreams.

WHERE YOUR STRENGTHS AND YOUR VALUES MEET

The places where your strengths and values intersect are especially powerful and magical. If you combine what you're brilliant at with what you're most passionate about, you have both the ability and the drive to create extraordinary results.

I invite you to take a look now at your list of strengths and your list of values. Ask yourself how you can bring them together in your personal and work life, or where there's scope to merge them to help you deal with difficult situations and to take advantage of new opportunities to identify and achieve goals.

For example, if one of your values is family, and one of your strengths is as a maximiser, why not ask yourself where there is scope to maximise your relationship with each member of your family – what projects, holidays, goals you can work on together as a family that you will all enjoy and feel inspired by?

Or if one of your values is being spiritual, and one of your strengths is communication, what would happen if you combined the two personally and professionally? So if you're a coach, for example, why not start a coaching programme aimed at clergy? Or you might consider taking a course in spiritual counselling.

While your needs will drain your energy if not met, identifying your values and making sure they are reflected in your goals, your choices and your approach to making positive change is energising. It is your secret ingredient for success.

———

FROM THEORY TO PRACTICE

One of my executive coaching clients, Tom, recently created some professional breakthroughs as a leader by understanding, leveraging, and juxtaposing his strengths and values. His company had just been through a restructure, morale was low and people were feeling generally demotivated and anxious. Understanding that one of his strengths was individualisation and another was as a communicator, and that his values included making a difference and loyalty, he created a new approach to developing his relationship with each team member by spending more time with them and understanding what they individually had to contribute and how they could be best encouraged. As a result of Tom's investment of time and energy, each team member felt recognised and motivated, and Tom was himself inspired by the difference he had made – individually and collectively – to the team's energy, engagement and renewed determination.

PUTTING IT ALL TOGETHER INTO YOUR ACTION PLAN

In this chapter, you've been rolling up your sleeves, doing some soul-searching, some thinking and reflection and some writing. So I hope by now you've come up with some clear insights into your personality type and how to be your best self and support yourself through change, what your needs are and how to get them met, what your key strengths are and how you might leverage them and what your top inspiring values are.

But how might all this work for you? Let's take the example of Sarah, a former freelance journalist and now a public relations consultant. In Sarah's first coaching session with me, she explained, tearfully, that she was disenchanted with her current career, unhappily single and was feeling lost in her own life.

We started our work together by establishing her Enneagram personality type, which was a Type 6, the Loyalist. Type 6s like structure, predictability and close support from people around them, as they are prone to anxiety, doubt and insecurity. Sarah's freelance position was actually negative for her on so many levels, working against her need for work and financial security. And her desire for close connection with colleagues was being frustrated by the solitary nature of being a freelance writer. We then identified her needs which included security, and being cherished, as well as prosperity and recognition. Clearly her current situation was not meeting her needs as well as being a poor fit for her Enneagram type.

Sarah and I also established that being single was

particularly challenging for her, given her personality and her needs, and that she needed to put more focus into her friendships in the meantime in order to feel happier and more secure.

We then identified Sarah's strengths, which included being a communicator, having a natural ability to charm people and connecting to create positive relationships. We discovered that her values included beauty, elegance and achieving.

Through several coaching conversations, we established that Sarah's vocation would include using her sales and relationship-building skills to attract and keep new clients in an environment which related to beauty, providing the opportunity to use her professional strengths to excel. Sarah decided that her ideal career would be working in a public relations consultancy specialising in fashion. We then helped her to get crystal clear on why she would make such a distinctive and valuable contribution in that area.

I am happy to say that she found exactly such a job where she has been extremely successful for the last two years, and that she is also now in a relationship with a man she adores. Her work and her life are both in a dramatically different and happier place than they were a few years ago, and all because she identified and leveraged her personality type, needs, values and strengths.

And you can do it too! If you haven't already done so,

why not now consolidate what you've learned and type it up into an A4 page blueprint. This page is your new treasure map. Equipped with a new understanding of the unique individual that you are, you now have all the ingredients for your own fabulous recipe for positive change.

In the next chapter, we will put everything you've learned so far together to create an action plan for surfing the waves of change.

———

CHAPTER 5

The Plan: Bringing It All Together

This is where everything gets really exciting! At this point, you're ready to combine all the steps you've taken so far to form the personally prescribed plan that will get you to where you want to go.

WHAT'S YOUR VISION NOW?

You're now ready to create a bigger, brighter, more luminous and exciting vision than you've ever had before – one that truly inspires and magnetises you forward to where

———

you want to be. Not only that, but it will also be more focused and precise, rather than hazy and vague. And the crystal clarity of your vision will, in turn, help you turn it into reality.

With your new understanding of your personality, needs and strengths, and having cleared some of the things and situations in your life that were draining your energy, you're now in a position to identify what your dream destination *really* looks like.

YOUR VISION DAY (PART TWO)

Let me invite you to schedule another exciting Vision Day just for you – a day you can devote to identifying and shining a light on the vision that represents what you want your life to look and feel like, where you want to be in your life and, more importantly, *who* you want to be in your life.

Have a look at your diary or calendar, and decide which day looks best to book for your Vision Day. Is it a Saturday or Sunday? Or do you want to organise a free day for yourself during the week? Whenever you decide to do it, the important thing is that you set it aside for yourself *completely* – that you don't do chores of any kind, you don't check your emails, chat with friends ... don't do anything except focus on your vision. Just like in your previous Vision Day (see p. 83), decide on the environment that will be most inspiring and uplifting, whether it's your garden or a park, your living room, a coffee shop, a museum; the main thing is that it's somewhere you feel comfortable, relaxed and happy.

Getting supplies for your Vision Day

Just as you did for your first Vision Day, make sure you've got your coaching notebook (or any notebook/paper you like the look of), coloured pens and pencils, any art supplies you feel like using (glitter, stickers, etc.) and a large piece of heavy white paper or card for a vision board.

Finding images

Your next step is to look through some magazines and cut out anything – words or pictures – that you're attracted to. Collecting images that represent what you're drawn to and what you want to achieve will help you to formulate your vision and create a vision board that will bring it to life. Look through your photo collection and pull out some photos of yourself looking happy and having fun. Search for images and words that truly inspire you. Choose magazines that make you feel good, perhaps some that are aspirational, as well as inspirational. When you see pictures, images, words that really appeal to you, cut them out and start a collection to represent aspects of your vision.

Reflecting and note-taking

Before your Vision Day, I suggest you prepare to get the most out of it by doing the following:

- **Reflecting on your personality type** What situations/circumstances/places/people bring out the best in you? What do you need to be your happiest?

- **Reflecting on your emotional needs** What has to be in place for you to feel satisfied, safe and content? Go into as much detail as you can.

- **Reflecting on your strengths** What are you naturally good at? Which strengths have helped you to work wonders in the past? Which strengths do you most enjoy using?

- **What makes you feel your most energised, vibrant self physically?** In terms of exercise, diet, lifestyle, activities, climate, scenery, work/life balance? Do you feel happiest in the sunshine, in the UK or abroad? In the country? In the city? Do you enjoy spending time with a few close friends? Or being part of a wider community? Do you feel more energised working in an office or at home? Do you prefer working on your own, or with colleagues?

- **What does spiritual fulfilment mean to you?** What needs to be in place for you to feel inspired spiritually, however you interpret that?

- **What stimulates and excites you mentally?** What kinds of conversations do you most enjoy having, and with whom? What kind of work do you find most interesting? What things do you like doing for fun that are mentally absorbing?

- Most importantly, consider your values ...

Your values and your vision

Your values are the most important element to consider when creating your vision, because they inspire and delight you, and if you juxtapose your values with your strengths, you've got a magical recipe for fulfilment, happiness and bliss.

Write down your top four values (those you identified in the previous chapter – see p. 169) on a sheet of paper, leaving enough space around each one to add drawings, doodles, other words, images, pictures, anything else that springs to mind. Write down your strengths underneath your values and practise combining each value with each strength. What pictures emerge? For example, if one of your values is adventure and one of your strengths is empathy, getting involved in some charity or volunteer work abroad could be a wonderful idea for you.

As you look at each value, why not get a little playful and imaginative? Imagine that your value is personified, standing in front of you as a character of some sort. Who might it be? What might it look like? Why not ask it where it would have you go, what it would have you do? For example, if you were to follow Adventure and go where it leads you, where would it take you? What is Adventure trying to say to you? Is it saying, 'Come with me on a round-the-world cruise?' Or is Adventure inviting you to shake up your routine completely, go to Cuba to learn salsa dancing, perhaps change your career or perhaps completely change your image?

After you've considered each value in depth and really listened to what it might be trying to say to you, record your insights in detail in your journal or notebook and, if you feel inspired to do so, draw any pictures that come to mind in relation to each value.

Get Ready, Set, Go!

You've now done your preparatory work – thinking, visualising, note-taking, collecting pictures. Hopefully, you have amassed notes and thoughts on things, experiences and qualities that really appeal to you and that represent aspects of your vision.

The next step is, in fact, to step back, and focus exclusively on your dream destination – on where you want to go, on what your vision actually might look like and might be.

At a recent coaching client retreat on the island of Capri, one memorable Saturday morning was devoted to identifying each person's vision and vision statement. We sat in the sunshine on the terrace of our hotel suite, gazing out at the sea and the Faraglioni rocks, getting more inspired by the minute. When I asked each person to close their eyes and imagine the most beautiful place they could in order to get them in the right frame of mind for finding their vision, they all laughed at me, and said they didn't need to close their eyes – they could just look around them, as they were already in the most gorgeous place imaginable! It's true that it helps to be in a breathtakingly beautiful location in order to be inspired to imagine beyond the possible to the seemingly impossible, so try to find the most inspiring location for your visioning that you can.

It's now time to start your Vision Day and enjoy the luxury of sustained time and focus to really develop your thinking and be as creative as you want to be.

Identifying and Understanding Your Vision: What to Do on Your Vision Day

Let's focus now on identifying and understanding your vision.

There are lots of ways into this. If you just want to launch yourself into imagining, go right ahead. You might want to look at your values, your notes on your needs, strengths and personality type and the pictures you've cut out too. But if you would prefer a more structured approach, why not start like this?

Get really comfortable and relaxed, perhaps with some herbal tea or coffee close at hand, perhaps listening to some music that makes you feel happy and/or inspired, perhaps doing some yoga or meditating first to still your mind, if that is something you enjoy ...

Now close your eyes (or look at the gorgeous view in front of you) and imagine where you really want to be in five years' time, in ten years' time. If anything was possible (and sometimes it is), if you weren't compromising in any way, where would you be and what would you be doing? Who would you be with? What would you look like? More importantly, how would you be feeling? What place can you see? What work would you be doing? What would your work/life balance look like?

For example, you might imagine yourself in a holiday

home on one of the Florida Keys, sitting by a private pool in a reclining chair, your partner sitting next to you doing the crossword, both of you drinking freshly squeezed orange juice and sparkling mineral water. You might be writing your next bestselling book, immersed, inspired, surrounded by hibiscus flowers, knowing that when you've finished your next chapter, you will both have a swim in your pool and then go inside for a shower and get changed to go out for cocktails and dinner on the beach.

You might imagine yourself working in your ideal job in London, meeting your partner for drinks at the end of the working day, then commuting back together to your happy home, watering your window boxes and making dinner together.

Write down everything that you see, and write down as many words as possible to describe how you're feeling in your vision. If you feel like drawing pictures, then do. Get as much down on paper as you can to convey your ideal future.

The idea here is to get beyond what you know intellectually: to centre yourself and create a still and peaceful inner feeling, to transcend the limitations of linear thinking and any habits of thought you may have and to identify colours, words, feelings, symbols and metaphors that speak to you.

The next step is to look at each of your values and ask what it can add to your vision. If you think about each one three-dimensionally, what is it telling you and how does it clarify and contribute to your vision? Read through all your notes, look at all your photos, quotes and pictures. What are they saying to you?

So what might your ten-year vision look like? Everyone's is different. One of the key things to ask yourself though is how you can make your vision as bright, shiny and compelling as possible. We can sometimes imagine something that doesn't represent what we truly long for. So it's useful to ask yourself if there's scope to amplify. Here's an example:

You might say your vision is that you work four days a week and have one day at home with your young family, that you have a closer relationship with your partner and that you have one holiday abroad each year. Now how could you enhance your vision even further, stretching your sense of what's possible? Let's try Take 2. Your vision might show you having your successful home-based business, taking your kids to school every day and picking them up, enjoying an inspiring home study with lovely views and beautiful art and travelling to appealing places for meetings with clients. That sounds better, doesn't it? Let's enhance it even further now and try Take 3. Your vision might include all the elements in the previous one, but also show you having a wonderfully romantic and connected relationship with your partner, living in a house with idyllic views in the country, enjoying two holidays a year, being financially comfortable, being at or close to your ideal weight and feeling glowing. And what might Take 4 look like?

Essentially, I'm asking you to shoot for the moon. After all, remember the saying that if you shoot for the moon and miss, you still might land on some stars . . .

Now here are some more questions to ask yourself in order to really capture the scope, scale and personality of your vision. You may have come across a few of these questions in previous chapters, but they are also relevant to this stage of your journey:

- What does your vision look like, feel like, sound like?

- What is your highest vision for your life?

- What is really important to you?

- What are the top five experiences you wish to create in your life?

- Who are your role models? Who are the real or fictional people, alive or dead, who have most inspired you so far in your life?

- What are your values and what are their implications for your life and work?

- What do you daydream about?

- Have you ever had a sense of a mission or purpose in

your life, waiting to be stepped into? What do you know about this? What do you sense about it?

- Consider your personal goals, your relationships, your family, your health, your finances, your career, your spirituality. What are they telling you about, and adding to, your vision?

- Where would you like to be ideally in five years' time? In ten years' time?

Once you're confident that you've identified all the elements and aspects of your vision, your next step is to try to encapsulate your vision of your dream destination in writing. Put together a paragraph that summarises the key qualities, experiences, achievements, ingredients of your vision.

Your vision statement

Now that you have expressed your vision in a paragraph, the next important and exciting step is to distil it into a single sentence. And not just any sentence, but one that is ten words long and, ideally, includes your values, or at least the essence of them.

An effective vision statement needs to:

- come from your heart and soul

- express you at your authentic best – the you that you will become

- be vivid, full of passion and positive emotion

- be driven by your values

- be inspired by your favourite quote or motto, or maybe reminiscent of your favourite children's book.

Essentially, your vision statement is your satellite navigation system, your GPS to get you exactly where you want to go. It should make you excited and charged up, fired up, ready to go!

Let me take you through the process of turning your vision paragraph into a vision statement. Suppose your paragraph states that your values are creativity, joy, nature, family, that you want a better work/life balance, to live by the sea, have more time and closeness with your family, do something creative that is also lucrative.

The first draft of your vision statement might read like this: 'I live a creative, joyful life by the sea, surrounded by my family, making a good living with my artwork.' That's twenty words and it's on the right track, but a bit clunky still. Let's make it more precise: 'My creative, stable family-centred life by the sea is joyful, balanced and prosperous.' That's fourteen words, so getting better, but still not as crystalline as it might be. Let's try again: 'I live a joyful creative prosperous family-centred life by the sea.' Twelve words – definitely getting there. Now one more try: 'My seaside life is joyful, family-centred, creative and prosperous.' Ten words and beautifully clear! Do you get the picture – literally?

Let's try another version. Suppose your four values are dynamism, success, balance and beauty. Perhaps in your vision paragraph you wrote that you wanted to combine your successful career in London with time in a beautiful home in the country, creating both balance and success in your life. Your vision statement might go something like this: 'My dynamic, successful urban career harmonises with my countryside idyll.'

Or perhaps your vision paragraph is about creating a balance between inspiring time alone and the spiritual with dynamic extroverted involvement in career and the world. Your vision statement might say, 'My life balances stillness and dance, reflection and dynamic exploration.'

If, for example, you have a more specific vision paragraph about living in a penthouse apartment in a city and having an exciting social life and community, your vision statement might go like this: 'I love my city penthouse and my fun, vibrant community.'

It also works well if you want to create a vision and a vision statement (and, ultimately a vision board, but more of that below) for just one aspect of your life – your love life or your career, for example.

Ultimately, whatever your vision and vision statement, creating one that is just perfect for you allows you to draw towards you the life that you want to live. It tells your brain what to look for and harnesses the power of intention and visualisation to work on your behalf. As I mentioned earlier, your vision statement works like a satellite navigation system, helping you stay on track as you progress to your dream destination, making sure that you don't get sidetracked, derailed or lost as you continue your journey. If you're headed for Las Vegas, you don't want to make a lengthy detour into the Nevada suburbs, after all. So what's *your* vision statement?

Your vision board

Well done for creating your clear vision and for distilling it into a vision statement. You now have a wonderful head start on translating your vision into reality. Your next step is to create a vision board which will be your visual reminder and signpost to where you are heading.

If you haven't already done so, it's now time to gather several magazines that appeal to you and represent different aspects of your dreams. Look through them and cut out all the pictures that appeal to you and symbolise feelings, qualities, experiences, things that you want to attract into your life. Try to go beyond the superficial to the essence and find pictures that convey the spirit and the quality of what you want for yourself and your life.

It is also helpful to collect words, phrases, expressions, quotes from movies, poetry or songs that verbally express aspects of your vision and to print them out ready to display on your vision board too. For example, I love *It's a Wonderful Life* – the Frank Capra classic starring Jimmy Stewart – and I'm sure those words will be on my next vision board. What are your favourite inspiring films or moments in films? Is there a song that in some way encapsulates your vision? Why not print out the most important words of the song? It might be, 'Don't Worry, Be Happy' or lyrics from the Beach Boys' 'Kokomo', for example. Which song lyrics are most enticing to you? Which represent how you want to live?

Finally, find a photo of yourself in which you look really happy, like the you that you want to be, and put that on your vision board too.

So if you're ready with your large piece of white card, a glue stick, some scissors, your pictures, words and printed out vision statement, let's get to work.

I suggest you put on some happy music in the background to make the whole process of creating your vision board as joyful as your journey has been towards bringing it to life. And, if you're so inclined, you might even light a candle or some incense, diffuse some essential oils (depending on your vision, maybe jasmine, sandalwood, geranium, lavender), and make yourself some tea (rose, green, Earl Grey) or other drink (champagne, espresso, mojito). Pay attention to exactly what appeals to you and resonates with your individual vision.

It's probably best to start by putting your vision statement in the middle of the board, along with your photo and your defining image – the one that most encapsulates your vision – then play around with the process of creation, making it fun and happy, as you stick the various words and pictures you've chosen around your vision statement. When you're happy with what you've produced, tell yourself, 'Well done', and display your vision board somewhere prominent where you'll see it as much as possible every day.

Your goals and your plan

Now that you have your vision board and statement, you need to use them to help you identify your goals and chart your goal calendar and plan. It's time to ask yourself if you want to make a five- or a ten-year plan. Considering your age and life situation right now, and the nature of your vision statement, which time frame is a better fit for you?

The ten-year vision

Let's start with getting clear on your ten-year dream destination. Given everything you've written so far, imagine yourself feeling incredibly happy, fulfilled, joyful in ten years' time. Look at your vision statement and your vision board and let's identify your ten-year goals: where, what and who do you want to be in ten years' time? What does living your dream mean to you? You need to know where and who you are at the moment, and where and who you want to be in order to make your plan to get from here to there. Are you ready to commit to your plan for your future? Are you really ready? Then let's go.

We'll start with an example. One of my clients recently identified the following things he wanted to have achieved in the ten-year timeframe. This is what he wrote:

- To be happily married

- To be healthy, fit, vibrant, at my physically energised best and at my ideal weight

- Balance and serenity

- A second home abroad, somewhere sunny and beautiful, to spend half the year in

- A wide circle of close friends

- Children – happy, healthy, with good jobs after

successful university and school experience

- Financial independence

Now let's imagine *your* ten-year vision. Why not write your key destination points below?

- _____
- _____
- _____
- _____
- _____
- _____
- _____

The five-year vision

If you choose to create a ten-year vision, let's look at who and where you need to be in five years' time in order to achieve it. What does the halfway point look like? Here's the five-year vision of the client whose ten-year vision we looked at above:

- Be happily married
- Healthy, fit, vibrant, at my physical best and ideal weight

- Balance and serenity
- Have second home abroad where I spend part of the year
- Children have done well at school, been accepted to their university of choice, are happy and healthy
- Have paid off mortgage and be on track with pension
- Successful business expansion: turnover doubled from current level
- Have a wide circle of friends

What do you notice about the visions? You will see that some of the points are the same, whereas others have been adjusted to reflect the shorter time scale: we still see the second home abroad, but he wants to spend part of the year there, instead of half the year; rather than financial independence, we see the intention to have paid off his mortgage and be on track with his pension.

Now look again at your own ten-year vision and decide what your five-year version needs to look like:

- _____

- _____

- _____

- _____

———

- _____

- _____

- _____

Well done! You must be getting more excited and happier by the minute as your dream destination vision becomes an increasingly tangible and accessible reality.

The one-year vision

Next, we'll create your one-year vision. Looking at your five-year vision, where do you need to be in a year's time to be on track to make it happen?

Let's go back to my client's example to get an idea of how to do it. Here's his one year vision:

- In happy relationship with person I will marry

- Healthy, fit, vibrant, at my physical best and ideal weight

- Have established yoga and meditation routine to create more balance and serenity

- Have a couple of new, close friends

- Children happy, healthy, preparing for successful GCSEs

- Research and identify where to buy my home abroad
- List places I want to travel to for holidays over the next several years
- Increase business turnover by 10 per cent

Do you see how the above goals are a modified, more approachable version of those in the five-year vision? If we take one strand of the vision, say, buying the holiday home abroad, the trajectory of goals, year by year, might look something like this:

- Year 10: own home abroad, somewhere sunny and beautiful, where I spend half the year
- Year 9: same
- Year 8: same
- Year 7: same, but spend less than half of the year there
- Year 6: as year 7
- Year 5: as year 7
- Year 4: buy second home abroad and take two holidays there; own mortgage almost paid off
- Year 3: visit homes abroad in destination of choice; decide on location and style of house
- Year 2: research destinations for buying home

---

abroad and visit them; decide on destination and research finance options

- Year 1: research destination for buying home abroad

Can you see how much more accessible and realistic this part of the vision is when you break it down into annual milestones? And the same is true for every one of your constituent goals. When looked at in terms of your ten-year vision, the goal may seem just too far out of reach. But if you break it down into annual milestones, suddenly you see that it is, in fact, achievable. Now you try it here:

- Year 10: _____
- Year 9: _____
- Year 8: _____
- Year 7: _____
- Year 6: _____
- Year 5: _____
- Year 4: _____
- Year 3: _____
- Year 2: _____
- Year 1: _____

Now that you have your one-year vision, it's time to make your one-year plan. But you've already achieved a tremendous amount in your Vision Day, so let's now call an end to your work for today and take some time to celebrate how far you've come! I think a celebratory evening out, a glass of champagne, a game of golf with the boys, or spa day out with the girls is called for! When you've celebrated suitably, you can begin work on your one-year plan.

CREATING YOUR ONE-YEAR PLAN

In order to bring your one-year vision to life and really make it happen, you need to break it down into month-size pieces. And you need to commit to working on your monthly goals in a focused and diligent way in order to achieve them. I suggest you start with twelve months and what needs to be in place by then, and work backwards. Here's the example from the same person we looked at earlier:

- Month 12: have achieved one-year vision by end of month 12. Celebrate!
- Month 11: shortlist destinations for holiday home and

decide on a short shortlist of two possibilities; enjoy everything I've achieved this year

- Month 10: more time enjoying relationship and friendships; more research on holiday home destinations; more business focus; continue healthy lifestyle habits

- Month 9: start researching possible destinations for holiday home; holiday planning; more time with kids

- Month 8: fine-tune plan for balance and serenity: (how are the yoga and meditation going), introduce regular massage, walk more in nature, start a journal, enjoy relationship; continue healthy lifestyle and training from 10km race

- Month 7: hope to be in happy new relationship by now if not sooner; if not, keep dating; continue active social life, time with kids, exercise and healthy eating; train for 10km race; assess business growth and make changes as necessary

- Month 6: actively cultivate new friendships; spend extra time with children and think about what they need to be their happiest and how I can support and encourage them academically

- Month 5: buy new clothes I feel great in; continue socialising and dating; start daily yoga and/or

meditation practice; continue healthy eating and
exercising; lose last four pounds

- Month 4: continue dating; join local club or evening
  class to meet new friends; assess business growth and
  see what else to do to grow turnover by 10 per cent
  this year; join or start a book club; continue healthy
  eating and exercise; lose four more pounds

- Month 3: start dating – plan couple of social activities
  to meet people each week; consider speed dating,
  Internet dating, agencies to meet more possible dates;
  continue exercise programme and healthy eating; lose
  another four pounds

- Month 2: lose four pounds; see nutritionist to get
  healthy diet and vitamin supplement advice; start
  weekly yoga/meditation class

- Month 1: make healthy eating and exercise plan; start
  weekly gym classes/exercising four times a week

Now have a go at creating your own one-year plan:

- Month 12: _____
- Month 11: _____
- Month 10: _____
- Month 9: _____

- Month 8: _____

- Month 7: _____

- Month 6: _____

- Month 5: _____

- Month 4: _____

- Month 3: _____

- Month 2: _____

- Month 1: _____

You should now be feeling focused and clear about how your monthly goals relate to your one-, five- and ten-year vision. Your next step is to break down your monthly goals into even more specific weekly steps. Let me show you what I mean from my client's Month 1 goals. By the end of the first month, he wanted to have made a healthy eating and exercise plan, and to have started exercising four times a week. So his weekly goals looked like this:

- Week 1: book an appointment with a recommended nutritionist or research healthy eating with books, magazines or the Internet; research gyms and bootcamp classes

- Week 2: create healthy eating plan; shortlist gyms and bootcamp classes
- Week 3: do first grocery shop to stock up for healthy eating/weight-loss plan; do trial visits for shortlisted gyms and bootcamps
- Week 4: begin healthy eating/weight-loss plan and take starting weight and measurements; join preferred gym or bootcamp and attend first class or session

Now, what about your weekly goals? What do they look like?

- Week 1: _____
- Week 2: _____
- Week 3: _____
- Week 4: _____

Counting backwards from your ten-year vision to your five- and then one-year vision allows you to identify the stepping stones and milestones that will take you where you want to go. It is very important that you record these, so that you have a visual reminder of where you're going and what you need to do to get there.

Many people find year-at-a-glance wall charts extremely helpful as visual prompts and focusing systems and I suggest you think about buying one, filling it in, and displaying it somewhere very visible, ideally close to your vision board. You might also try a goal calendar with a month and a week at a glance – ideally something big enough that you can itemise each baby step to take you where you want to go.

HOW TO KEEP ON TRACK

Here are some useful pointers to help you move successfully towards achieving your one-year vision:

- Check in with yourself. Once you have identified your weekly goals, schedule a weekly check-in meeting with yourself, to ensure that you're on track. If you're working with a coach, then your coach will keep you moving forward, give you accountability and help with your motivation. If you don't have a coach, why not team up with a friend or two and support each other on this adventure, perhaps meeting in your local coffee shop once a week to chart your progress? If you prefer to simply have your weekly check-in meeting with yourself, that's fine too, and I suggest you choose the same time each week, so you can turn it into a habit and part of your ongoing routine. Sunday evening works well as it's a naturally reflective time; it's also the end of one week and the start of another, which encourages you to keep perspective and maintain the forward momentum.

- Ask yourself, 'What is my one next step today?' (and make sure it's clearly defined). What do you need to do today to achieve your weekly and your monthly goal? And when are you going to do it?

- Keep your dream destination, your ten-year vision, in your daily awareness so you can allow its inspiration to magnetise you forward.

- Make sure your vision board is somewhere really visible so you can see it every day as a visual reminder of where you're heading. Maybe even consider making a mini vision board as well, perhaps a postcard size image or a bookmark, so you can carry your vision in your pocket at all times!

- Look after yourself on this journey of change. It can be challenging and difficult to let go of the past and move steadfastly through from where you are to where you want to be. Are you practising wonderful self-care? What are you doing for yourself every day that makes you feel good and energises you? Create a feeling-good plan you can practise daily, so that the journey itself is as pleasurable as the destination.

- Live in the present. Don't allow your vision of where you want to go to distract you from living fully immersed in today; make sure that you enjoy each present moment too.

- Keep positive! Check in daily to make sure that you are talking to yourself in a positive and encouraging way, and if you're not, then turn your self-talk around each time you catch yourself saying something discouraging. Most of us are much nicer to our friends than we are to ourselves; you need to be your own best cheerleader, so keep up with the positive self-talk until it becomes a habit.

- And talking of cheerleaders, make sure that you have a small group of supportive friends and family around you, to whom you can report progress and who will cheer you on and encourage you.

- Get more information when you need to. Some of your goals may require a bit of research or investigation to achieve properly. Do it!

- Take baby steps. Don't be overwhelmed by the big gap between where you are now and where you want to be. If you focus on the gap, you may feel paralysed or overwhelmed. A marathon starts with a single step, so focus on the one next step you can take today. And tomorrow and next week, focus on the next ones. You will get to where you want to go by breaking it into smaller chunks.

- Get started! Don't wait for the perfect moment – it may never arrive. Perfectionism can be a real problem and can stop you before you've even got going. So lower your standards and start today. If, for example, you want to write the first chapter of your book, don't feel like you have to write the perfect chapter today. Instead, tell yourself you can start with an outline, or a very rough draft, and that you can then fine-tune and polish it.

- Don't sabotage yourself. You know how you can get in your own way; be clear about what's happening, and make sure that you don't do that.

- Forgive yourself. If you miss a day or week or month because of everyday life getting in your way, don't use that as an excuse to step off your pathway to your dream destination. Pick yourself up and carry on from where you left off. If you're trying to lose weight, for example, you wouldn't want to quit your healthy-eating plan just because you enjoyed a cream cake accidentally on purpose!

- And, perhaps most importantly, reward yourself! For each mini (and big) milestone you achieve, make sure you take time out to celebrate your progress. Go out for dinner with friends; have a glass of champagne;

buy a special cake; go for a celebratory spa trip or golf game. The main thing is to encourage yourself at each step of your journey. Think about it . . . in a football game, we don't sit silently until the game is won, but we cheer for each goal and good play. We don't just water a rose when it's flowered! Watering it along the way will create a bigger and more beautiful flower. And you need to celebrate each individual step or mini milestone along your journey to living your dreams. Doing so will accelerate your progress, as well as keeping you motivated, focused and positive.

Creating your vision and then your plan allows you to commit to creating a fabulous day, week, month, year and, ultimately, a wonderful life. You get to choose the kind of route you want to take: a road to nowhere or a path to an extraordinary life and the destination of your dreams.

Each choice you make can positively alter the direction of your life. And, after all, what you see depends on what you look for. Creating your vision and your ten-/five-/one-year plan is, ultimately, about actively and deliberately choosing to *lead* your life: deciding who you want to be, and then carving out the life that allows you to be that person. Everything you do, every choice you make is geared towards that positive outcome.

CHAPTER 6

The End is Where
We Start From

Welcome to wonderland! You have been on an exciting, sometimes scary, sometimes challenging, adventure of change as you've been reading and working through this book.

We have looked at what happens when you go through change and transitions, whether this is something that is externally imposed upon you that you then have to

---

navigate, or whether it's a change you instigate yourself. We have explored how change is actually an invitation to a journey – a journey of self-discovery and initiation into new insights, experiences, aspects of yourself, ultimately even a deeper understanding of how you want your life to reflect the you that you really are, the you you want to be.

We have spent time creating a road map with practical steps to get you from where you are, where you started this exploration, to where you want to be, your dream destination. We've looked at the shape of your journey towards change, the landmarks you can expect (and prepare yourself for) on the path, and insights to take with you. We've also explored the steps to creating clarity about your dream destination: understanding yourself and your personality, identifying and eliminating energy drains, defining your needs and getting them met, analysing your strengths and working out how to leverage them and exploring your key values – the themes that most inspire you and radiate brilliance into your life.

As you go through your own journey of change, you will notice (whether at the time or in retrospect) the various stages and the particular challenges and opportunities they bring with them.

———

THE SEVEN STAGES OF CHANGE AND TRANSITION

Working with coaching clients through transition over the years, I've identified seven discernible stages of change:

1. Here, you are entrenched in your life, perhaps feeling a bit bored, stultified, blocked, but essentially you're closed to questioning and are just getting on with it, even if you don't feel as full of life and excitement as you might.

2. In stage two, you are still in this stuck, fixed place, but you are beginning to ask questions, such as: 'Is this all there is?'; 'Is this career really what I want to be doing for the rest of my life?'

3. Here, you are beginning to feel distinctly unsettled and restless. Either you sense that an external change is about to be imposed upon you (perhaps your company has just announced a significant lay-off/redundancy programme, for example) or you feel an inner restlessness and call to adventure that tells you change has to be imminent. At this point, though, you're still feeling a bit stuck and blocked, and are not sure if you do want to change or how you will go about it.

---

4. You now know that you either need to change or you want to, and you start preparing yourself to leave the familiar and start your journey, whether the change is desired or catapulted upon you. So you might, for example, be in a situation where your partner has left you, and you might be feeling shocked and devastated, still holding on to the reality that you thought you were living in, but aware that it is already quite different from what you thought it was.

5. This is where you leave the known reality and start journeying into the unknown. You may well feel confused, in the dark, unable to see your way forward. These feelings are all completely natural and are a predictable and, actually, positive stepping stone on the journey from your old self and life to the new. You might feel a bit like Alice falling down the rabbit hole – 'curiouser and curiouser'. One expression for this betwixt-and-between phase is 'liminal'. It is when you've left your place of origin and are travelling to a new destination, even if you can't yet see (and you probably can't – certainly not at the beginning) where you're headed. For example, if you leave your job with a view to a career change, you might spend several months reflecting on what your true vocation is. This period between leaving and beginning could be called

liminal. It's a bit 'eye of the storm', in terms of feelings, and this book has held your hand, metaphorically, to show you how to navigate the rapids, so that you can clarify where you want to go and how to get there.

6. In stage six, you're still liminal, but have now identified your ideal destination, you've got a map and a compass, and you're heading towards a particular place. It's still scary, but you don't feel totally lost any more and you're moving confidently towards your new beginning.

7. Hurray! Your boat has arrived. You're now at your new destination and the you that is there is different from the you that left your place of origin. You now need to reintegrate yourself, understand what you've learned on your journey and how to use the treasures that you've discovered to infuse your life with their energy and power.

You can't get to where and who you want to be without going through the difficult times. Often your most profound learning and insights will emerge from the trials you encounter as you journey across the sea of change. You need to continue despite the inevitable setbacks, embrace change and move through it with faith and confidence in order to achieve your vision. By the time you get to the last stage, where your boat reaches its destination, you will be transformed as a result of your journey and will have learned about who you are and what you need to be happy.

ENDINGS AND BEGINNINGS

Flow into the knowledge that what you are seeking finishes often at the start, and, with ending, begins.

RAINER MARIA RILKE

Actually, the journey to change starts with an ending. Something in your life has to end and you have to let go of it, so that you can embark on the journey through the murky forest to create your wonderful new beginning. As Rilke so beautifully puts it above, what you are looking for 'finishes often at the start', rather like the Ouroboros symbol of the serpent whose tail is in its mouth, to form a perfect circle. Or as Frost says in his poem 'Directive', you need to be 'lost enough to find yourself'.

Like the mythical phoenix, the Ouroboros represents infinity or wholeness, something that recreates itself. Jung also saw the Ouroboros as a mandala symbol, reflecting man's integration and assimilation of the shadow side. It's

an alchemical symbol, showing a magically enriching individuation process leading us through change to a deeper,
truer, brighter and wiser new self and new life.

In 'God Give Me Strength', Elvis Costello and Burt
Bacharach write poignantly:

> ... I'm lost in imagining ...
> As I tumble back down to the earth.

What does this mean if you're currently feeling a bit like
Alice, falling vertiginously down a mysterious rabbit hole,
in the process of change which feels scary, maybe even
terrifying?

I think it means that if you are open to the insights and
understandings created through change, if you are lost
enough to find yourself, you can have faith that even the
dark places can lead you somewhere luminous and beautiful. You are able to learn what your shadow side is trying
to tell you, understand your values and your fears more
clearly and move forward to a new wonderland in the real
world you live in. If you learn who you really are, who you
really want to be, you can go on the journey of change
towards a new beginning, one which can be the life that
you dream of in your happiest dreams.

Just like the Ouroboros connects with itself to form a perfect circle, change can force you to connect with yourself, so

that you understand what you want, what you left behind and what you want to start in a new, more enlightened and more inspired way.

HOW TO NAVIGATE THE RAPIDS – OR LIFE SURFING

The best way to negotiate the rapids of change, is to step up and into them, using the waves to take you forward into your potential. Just like a surfer, go with the energy of the wave, rather than fighting it and becoming overwhelmed and going under. But what does this mean practically? It means allowing yourself to let go of the element in your life that has ended or that you've outgrown. It means allowing your journey to start with an ending, accepting that ending (even though this is much easier said than done) and giving yourself permission to explore and tolerate not knowing where you're going while you get more clarity on where you really *want* to go.

Of all the types of life changes you may have to go through, the two most likely scenarios concern work or relationships. My coaching clients usually present themselves with changes in one and sometimes both of these areas. Let's look at each in turn.

———

Work changes

Whether you decide proactively that you're unhappy in your job and that you want to change positions, or even career, or whether a change is forced upon you through redundancy, for example, the implications can be dramatic.

Whatever your work challenge, I know it's possible to create an extraordinarily happy and fulfilling work future for yourself that wonderfully reflects the individual you are. Let me share some examples of clients who have transformed their work satisfaction.

When Sue started coaching with me, she was married with two school-age children and had been out of the workforce for several years. She knew she felt bored and unfulfilled, missed her previous management-consultant career, but equally knew she didn't want to go back to that kind of work. And not having colleagues or intellectual stimulation was beginning to make her feel quite flat.

Over the course of our year working together, we clarified what her ideal work would look like, and realised that, in fact, she preferred to start her own business that she could work flexibly around her children, rather than go back into a more conventional corporate set-up. We also brainstormed the kind of work that most appealed to her, and the avenues suggested by her values: beauty, making a difference, harmony, creativity. Finally, we looked at her strengths to see where they intersected with her values, and thought about the practical lifestyle criteria that needed to be considered to create the best fit.

Sue was thrilled to come up with a business idea and plan for creating an interior design consultancy based on lifestyle: she took a course to give her the skills and practical knowhow and then started her new business, throwing a party to celebrate. Two years on, her business is thriving and her work satisfaction and sense of accomplishment are a vital part of her overall happiness and high energy. She comes across as a happy, dynamic, confident person, in a very different place from where she was before she discovered her vocation. And you can do this too!

Another client had a work transition forced upon him when he was made redundant from his director-level job at a creative company in London. Because of the coaching work we had already done together, Steve decided to view the change as a positive opportunity for growth, and he already had a clear idea of what an ideal path forward might look like, having a good understanding of his personality, needs, values and strengths. So he negotiated a good redundancy package, took six months off to travel the world and before he left on his travels, secured a CEO role at an exciting new company in Luxembourg, planning to divide his time between there and London. Rather than feel slighted or defeated by losing his job, Steve took the challenge and turned it into an opportunity for positive change. A year later, he enjoys his new supportive colleagues and the atmosphere of growth in the new company; he also loves his more cosmopolitan international lifestyle.

Steve is a great example of someone who took what is often perceived as a challenging work loss and turned it into a positive work development to enhance his happiness and lifestyle.

Relationship changes

Whether it's a question of improving communication, negotiating different needs or something intrinsically more challenging, like your partner's commitment issues or infidelity, your personal relationships provide one of the most testing, yet rewarding playgrounds for transformation. Relationship challenges force you to pay attention to yourself, your needs, your feelings and, ultimately, who you really are and what you want. It may well be that you picked up this book either because you want to initiate change within your relationship, or because your partner is forcing an externally imposed change upon you. Either way, the opportunity is there for transformation, growth and fulfilment, whether that's through improving your relationship and connecting to love more deeply, or stepping out of the relationship and rediscovering and reinventing yourself.

Relationship break-ups, divorce or bereavement can catapult us suddenly into dramatic, externally imposed call-to-adventure change. And relationship breakdowns can lead to personal breakthroughs, as I've seen with many clients. Over the years, several of my clients have initiated divorces from unhappy marriages and have emerged from the confusing and painful journey ultimately clearer, stronger and happier, while others have themselves been left by their partners, but have discovered, in the process, qualities in themselves they didn't know they possessed – a strength and centredness that has propelled them forward into a far happier and more fulfilling life.

Kate, for example, moved to England from Canada with her husband a few years ago, and gave up her high-powered job in Montreal in order to support her husband's career. One day, she went downstairs to breakfast to see a note on the table telling her that her husband had left her for another woman and that he would be in touch in a few months to sort out the divorce and the finances. As if that wasn't shocking enough, she found out over the next week that her husband had taken most of the money out of their bank accounts, including Kate's own accumulated savings. Reeling with shock, hurt and betrayal, Kate found herself in a foreign country with no job, no support network and very little money. Most of the things that defined her identity had disappeared, almost literally overnight.

Kate then attended an international group meeting in London where I was speaking about successfully navigating change. We talked, started working together and, a year later, Kate had a new job, a new group of fun and interesting friends and had created a community and security for herself from the inside out. Even though the previous year had been extremely challenging, especially the first few months, like Persephone coming out from the darkness of the underworld to a new spring, Kate rediscovered and recreated herself. On the other side of change, Kate was stronger, happier, wiser and more secure, with a clear plan on how to be her unique best self, and what brought out her best. She also knew the warning signs of traps and triggers to watch out for, things that might rear up out of nowhere, like a snake in a game of snakes and ladders, propelling her back down several rungs. Her new-found lucidity and self-awareness gave her an extraordinary centredness, energy and power to define and create the happy life she longed for.

WHO DO YOU WANT TO BE?

So here we are, back at the eponymous question. Once you determine to save your own life and follow your call to

———

adventure, nothing can ever be exactly the same again.

It's not just about knowing what you have to *do* on your journey but, more importantly, who you want to be. And by that I'm not recommending that you try to be someone else, someone other than yourself. On the contrary, I'm suggesting that you work diligently to understand who you really are, who you can be and who you *will* be when you're being your best, highest self. Because that is the real you. The work that you've done over the course of your journey with the help of this book will have given you an understanding of your personality type, your needs, your strengths and your values, as well as the information and perspective you need to deliberately express the essential you.

So to 'save' your life you must also understand who you are and make sure your life reflects and supports your best self.

If you understand yourself deeply, you can choose to live your life in a way that expresses who you are and what you want. Understanding who you are and ensuring that your life reflects you at your best also gives you integrity. By this, I mean being joined up and connected with yourself, so that everything you are and do is moving in the same direction – your life, thoughts, feelings, actions and words are all congruent and consistent with each other. So if you say you're going to do something, you're someone who can be relied upon to follow through and actually do it. You are someone others can trust. It means that your body, heart, mind and spirit are all doing the same thing, connecting with each other, and allowing you to be literally whole-hearted in the way you live your life and conduct yourself. If you're divided and split, you're by definition confused, disempowered and weak.

Then there is authenticity. This is quite close to integrity, but if integrity means wholeness, authenticity is about truthfulness. It's about being true to yourself, which really means honouring yourself, getting your needs taken of, respecting yourself in your self-talk and treating yourself kindly, not like an undeserving relative. Authenticity is about stepping out into the light of your unique best self and not compromising by living your second-best life.

Ask yourself then: what does my unique best self look like? What helps me to bring out my absolute best and what do I need to do to be that way more consistently? What traps do I need to watch out for and how can I avoid falling into them again? Being consciously aware of what to do and what to avoid – specifically, what will help or harm you – allows you to practise positive behaviour strategies and approaches until they become almost automatic.

Purpose and meaning

Understanding your vision, your values and your personality type (see Chapters 4 and 5) allows you to define your purpose and direction in life and to understand what creates meaning for you. Having a sense of what matters most and what you're here to do will guide you through all kinds of days and experiences, giving you a light on which to focus and around which to contextualise everything else. Equally, not having a sense of purpose, vision, direction and focus will cause you to waste time. Not having clearly defined goals can make you strangely loyal to performing daily acts of trivia – time wasting, in other words, which is strangely time consuming! Having fun and enjoying yourself, even if it's not focused or productive, is never a waste of time. But spending hours channel-surfing on the television or days running through small tasks on your to-do list that need to be done, (but not at the expense of working on the bigger picture of your life) isn't the most productive or inspiring use of time or your life!

A well-identified purpose and meaning allow you to create a clear intention for yourself, and focusing on your intention is the first and most powerful step in turning it into reality. As Ralph Waldo Emerson says, 'Once you make a decision, the universe conspires to make it happen'.

SYNCHRONICITY

It's extraordinary but true how identifying your vision and your intention can create remarkable synchronicity and success. At a recent coaching retreat in Capri, we spent a morning clarifying everyone's visions and vision statements – an inspiringly beautiful activity to do as part of a supportive group. A month later, Rachel, one of the participants emailed me to say this:

> It works! I was a bit sceptical initially, but now I'm a
> fully paid-up believer! Things are falling into my lap
> and I'm getting new business left, right and centre.
> And despite being so busy, I feel quite calm and
> serene! Having the time in Capri to sit and focus was
> so helpful and the vision stuff is so powerful. Wow!

Over my years of coaching, I have seen so many incredible examples of synchronicity that I have learned to see apparent coincidence as no coincidence at all. Whether you want to call it the Law of Attraction (what you focus on expands), or be more pragmatic and say that if you are focused and look for opportunities, they will present themselves, it doesn't really matter. But just as in the example of Rachel above, and how astonished she was to have had things, as she put it, fall 'into my lap' in the month after our Vision Day in Capri, it seems that when we get out of our own way and rid ourselves of energy drains, focusing positively on where we want to head and taking steps in that direction, the universe conspires to give us a helping hand.

I see so many examples of *seemingly* bizarre synchronicities with my coaching clients that it would be hard to pick just one, but it's often about being in the right place at the right time to meet the right person, seize the perfect opportunity, read just the right article. It's about showing up for your life. It's about grace too – however you account for it and whatever your own spiritual framework. One of my clients recently met and fell in love with someone she met on a train – and all because she stayed late at work to help a colleague through a professional crisis and ended up getting a later train home than normal. Her new partner is sure that someone or something 'up there' intervened to bring the two of them together.

The bottom line appears to be that the universe, fate, magic – whichever word you want to use – will intercede to move things around to help you and open doors in extraordinary ways, if you do your bit first. It's almost as if positive change happens because of a partnership between you and whatever good things are out there, and that if you take the step in front of you, the next step then becomes apparent. Knowing where you're heading and having a clear vision, direction and focus definitely facilitates this kind of co-operation or synchronicity, however you choose to account for it.

Embrace Change

Faith is sometimes defined as a belief in things unseen – we are invited to believe without seeing actual proof. It can be challenging to suspend disbelief when you're feeling anxious and scared, difficult to know that your wishes will come true when as yet you can't see any actual proof. Yet focusing on the positive and on what you want opens up a pathway along which you can walk towards it. Having faith in your ability to create the life you most desire, and believing in life's ability to support you in this creation is extraordinarily powerful and uplifting.

Magical helpers

In fictional calls to adventure and journeys towards change, the hero or heroine are often accompanied and assisted by a magical helper. In *The Hobbit* and *Lord of the Rings*, for example, the hobbit is helped by the wizard, Gandalf, the Elves of Rivendell and a mysterious bear/man, among others. In *The Wizard of Oz*, Glinda the Good Witch steps in to help Dorothy.

In your own quest, as you follow your call to adventure, you will encounter your own magical helpers, who will not be all they seem! On some level, we all know that we can't navigate our journey through change on our own, that our dark night of the soul needs a helpful – maybe magical – presence to illuminate it and show us the way. It may be that you happen to sit next to a stranger on a plane journey, just when you are feeling most alone and confused, and that stranger tells you just what you need to know at just the right time, before disappearing into the Arrivals Hall; or perhaps you're working with an inspiring coach who catalyses and supports you going forward; or you may have a chance conversation at the theatre one night that makes all the difference. Whatever the circumstances, chances are that you will come across your own magical helpers over the course of your journey.

To illustrate, let me tell you a true story about one of my own magical helpers. A long time ago, when I was getting divorced, I went to an Angel workshop in Bristol with angelologist and bestselling author Doreen Virtue. I was worried about my son, who was six at the time, anxious about the effects of the divorce on him, as he has always been an especially sensitive child. It was a large workshop with a few hundred people, and I sat somewhere near the back of the room, not knowing or talking to anyone. At one point, Doreen Virtue announced that she had recently developed some special cards called Unicorn Cards for children. Each card in the box had a special message on it and a picture of a unicorn, and they were designed, she explained, to help give children reassurance and comfort in times of stress or transition – times when they might have unanswered questions. I immediately thought of my son and felt that he would really enjoy using the cards. But imagine my surprise when Doreen suddenly said: 'Is there someone in the room called Nicole or Nicola? She has long blonde hair, and has a child who would benefit from these cards at this time.' I stood up, and she said, 'Yes, it's you.' She gave me the cards and said, 'These are for your child.' My son has loved having the cards for the last several years and they've been of great help to him.

Doreen definitely qualifies as a magical helper, as do Jim Cogan, my favourite teacher at Westminster School, and Frank Morral, my wise colleague, who taught alongside me at Carlton College in the USA and introduced me to the Enneagram. And I'm happy to say I have other magical helpers now.

Of course, in all the quest and adventure stories, as well as magical helpers, allies or supporters, there are also villains, obstacles, detractors who make your journey more arduous, and it's your job to watch out for them; be alert and make sure they don't tempt you off your chosen path into other distractions or dangers.

YEARLY PLAN:
THIS QUEST AND THE NEXT

In Chapter 5, we looked at defining your ten-year vision, then considering the five- and one-year versions. I suggest that every year you look again at what you've accomplished in the previous year and what you've achieved in relation to your one-year plan. It is then useful and timely to revisit your five-year plan, check that you are on track and that your plan is still relevant, right and sufficiently focused. It's a good idea to look back at the previous year on a chilly December afternoon, when you're ensconced somewhere cosy, and in a contemplative frame of mind. December lends itself naturally to reflection and assessment, just as January is conducive to looking at the new year ahead and fine-tuning your goals.

In essence then, remember to check your one-year plan each year and make sure you are still on track and moving forward, as well as revisiting, and, if necessary, adjusting your five-year vision and plan. Why not, in fact, make a diary note for each new year to assess your plans and see if you're where you want to be and what changes you may need to make?

LIVING YOUR DREAM

I hope you are now feeling excited about your own fantastic future, and the prospect of reaching your dream destination. Just as so many other people have done, you can follow your call to adventure, embark on your journey of change, and make your own way through the dark forest to harmony and bliss on the other side.

Anything can happen if you let it. Sometimes, difficult feelings and painful times will need to be moved through and lived, rather than avoided. I'm reminded of the well-known children's book, *We're Going on a Bear Hunt*, by Michael Rosen, which I read to my son when he was a toddler; there are times when you simply can't go under, over or around an obstacle, and that's when you'll realise, quite simply, 'Oh no, we've got to go through it!'

This book has given you the framework and the tools to make your call to adventure – this demand to 'go through it' – the start of a wonderful exploration towards happiness, your own unique quest. Your new beginning awaits you, shimmering invitingly right in front of you, and I know you're brave and strong enough to move towards it and, ultimately, to reach it.

I wish you joy, courage, perseverance and every happiness in this quest, and the next. I know you can become the you you were meant to be – that you can embrace change and enjoy your journey towards your dream destination.

As the poet E. E. Cummings writes:

Listen: there's a hell of a good universe next door; let's go.

RESOURCES AND
RECOMMENDED READING

Resources

If you are looking for a coach, I suggets you identify a credentialled coach from the International Coach Federation (ICF), the regulatory body for the coaching profession.

The International Coach Federation (ICF)
www.coachfederation.org

Coach University
www.coachu.com

The Enneagram Institute
www.enneagraminstitute.com

Recommended Reading

Buckingham, Marcus, *Now Discover Your Strengths*. Pocket Books, 2005

Buckingham, Marcus, *Go Put Your Strengths To Work*. Simon & Schuster, 2008

Goldberg, Michael J., *The Nine Ways of Working: How To Use The Enneagram To Discover Your Natural Strengths And Work More Effectively*. Marlowe & Co, 1999

Maitri, Sandra, *The Spiritual Dimension of The Enneagram: Nine Faces Of The Soul*. Jeremy P Tarcher, 2002

Riso, Don and Hudson, Russ, *The Wisdom Of The Enneagram*. Bantam, 1999

Riso, Don, *Enneagram Transformations*. Houghton Mifflin, 1996

CONTACT NICOLA

For more information about Nicola and her work, please visit her website: www.la-vita-nuova.com.

Nicola can be contacted via email: nicola@la-vita-nuova.com, or by telephone on 0845 222 0258.

If you would like to receive Nicola's free, inspirational monthly newsletter, please sign up via her website. You will also receive a complimentary three-part audio series.

You can also follow Nicola on Twitter: @LVNCoaching.

INDEX

Index

Index